But Is It All True?

But Is It All True?

The Bible and the
Question of Truth

Edited by

Alan G. Padgett *and* Patrick R. Keifert

WILLIAM B. EERDMANS PUBLISHING COMPANY
GRAND RAPIDS, MICHIGAN / CAMBRIDGE, U.K.

Wm. B. Eerdmans Publishing Co.
255 Jefferson Ave. S.E., Grand Rapids, Michigan 49503 /
P.O. Box 163, Cambridge CB3 9PU U.K.

Printed in the United States of America

11 10 09 08 07 06   7 6 5 4 3 2 1

Library of Congress Cataloging-in-Publication Data

But is it all true? the Bible and the question of truth /
  edited by Alan G. Padgett and Patrick R. Keifert.
      p.   cm.
  Includes bibliographical references.
    ISBN-10 0-8028-6316-7 / ISBN-13 978-0-8028-6316-4 (pbk.: alk. paper)
  1. Bible — Evidences, authority, etc.   2. Truth — Religious aspects — Christianity
  I. Padgett, Alan G., 1955- II. Keifert, Patrick R., 1950-

  BS480.B88   2006
  220.1'3 — dc22

                                            2005034138

www.eerdmans.com

O praise the LORD, all ye nations;
praise him, all ye people.
For his merciful kindness is great toward us;
and the truth of the LORD endureth for ever.
Praise ye the LORD.

Psalm 117

Contents

Acknowledgments

The authors and editors are grateful to the Lilly Foundation for funding the original colloquium, entitled "The Bible and Truth," which was the seed of this present volume. This grant was part of a larger research project headed by Donald Juel and Patrick Keifert, who have been enthusiastic leaders, supporters, and participants in this conversation. Important assistance for the completion of the editorial work was provided by research assistants Chelsea DeArmond and Judy Stack-Nelson, and also Chris Davis, as well as Sarah Dahl, who compiled the indexes. Thanks to Victoria Smith, faculty secretary at Luther Seminary, who read over every chapter with care. We also thank Reinder Van Til and Jon Pott of Eerdmans Publishing, our long-suffering editors, for their encouragement over the years. Finally, we would like to thank Kristen Esther Olson for asking her daddy the key question that describes our project, and thus for giving us the title for our book.

Although all the chapters in this book were written especially for this volume, some have already appeared elsewhere. The chapter by Mark Wallace was published as "The Rule of Love and the Testimony of the Spirit in Contemporary Biblical Hermeneutics," in *Between the Human and the Divine: Philosophical and Theological Hermeneutics,* edited by Andrzej Wiercinski (Toronto: The Hermeneutic Press, 2002), pp. 280-91. An earlier version of Dennis Olson's chapter was given as his inaugural address at

Princeton Theological Seminary, and published as "'Oh LORD God, How Am I to Know?'" *Princeton Seminary Bulletin* 23 (2002), 86-99. Our thanks to the authors and editors for permission to reprint them in the present collection. We also wish to note that the chapter by Stephen Davis will form a part of his volume *Christian Philosophical Theology* (Oxford University Press, forthcoming).

Contributors

DAVID BARTLETT is Lantz Professor of Preaching and Communication and Dean of Academic Affairs, Yale University Divinity School, New Haven, Connecticut.

ELLEN T. CHARRY is Margaret W. Harmon Associate Professor of Systematic Theology, Princeton Theological Seminary, Princeton, New Jersey.

STEPHEN T. DAVIS is Russell K. Pitzer Professor of Philosophy, Claremont McKenna College, Claremont, California.

PATRICK R. KEIFERT is Professor of Systematic Theology at Luther Seminary; and Director of Research, Church Innovations Institute, Saint Paul, Minnesota.

BEN C. OLLENBURGER is Professor of Biblical Theology, Associated Mennonite Biblical Seminary, Elkhart, Indiana.

DENNIS T. OLSON is Professor of Old Testament, Princeton Theological Seminary, Princeton, New Jersey.

ALAN G. PADGETT is Professor of Systematic Theology at Luther Seminary, Saint Paul, Minnesota.

MARK I. WALLACE is Associate Professor of Religion, Swarthmore College, Swarthmore, Pennsylvania.

NICHOLAS WOLTERSTORFF is Noah Porter Professor of Philosophical Theology, Emeritus, Yale University Divinity School, New Haven, Connecticut.

Introduction

ALAN G. PADGETT AND
PATRICK R. KEIFERT

I

This book came out of a deceptively simple question: When we say that the Bible is true, what do we mean? We first wrote most of the chapters that appear in this volume for a colloquium on the "Bible and Truth" at Azusa Pacific University in January 1999. We asked philosophers, biblical scholars, and theologians to answer this question — or a related one. We were particularly grateful to have such fine teachers and scholars read one another's work and enter into fruitful conversation. The colloquium was excellent, and the dialogue was rich and thought-provoking. We renewed old friendships and made new ones. We also had a wonderful time, and our thanks to APU, its administration and staff, for hosting us. Funding for the colloquium came from a larger grant and joint research project (of which Patrick Keifert will speak below). We are also grateful to the Lilly Endowment, Inc., for its support of our colloquium.

Over the years, these chapters have been revised and updated in the light of that conversation. We also invited new colleagues to contribute to our volume. We believe that the result of this collaborative project is a unique multidisciplinary reflection and dialogue, grounded in Christian faith and scholarship, on the question of truth in Scripture, including its interpretation and its theological confession today. Sadly, Donald H. Juel passed away in 2003, before this volume could be completed; he was to have been the co-editor. We dedicate this volume to his memory. He was a most excellent scholar, friend, and teacher of the church who graciously gave of his energy and spirit toward the completion of this project. We share with him a hope in the promise of God grounded in Christ's resurrection; and we know that in the Lord our labor is not in vain (1 Cor. 15:58).

Our culture's postmodern turn has raised in a new and powerful way the question of truth. It is not just academic philosophers who are pondering that ancient question: what is truth? The blurring of boundaries between fact and fiction, reality and imagination, is a fascinating aspect of current culture in the West. People begin to learn their history from fiction novels, as the *Da Vinci Code* phenomenon makes plain. The so-called news on our televisions seems closer to entertainment than facts. Some young people spend more of their free waking hours with virtual reality games, computers, and television than they do in the "real world." In the world of religion, despite the real differences between the great world faiths, a kind of lazy relativism seems to be the default view of a growing number of otherwise thoughtful people in the West. We can agree with Brian Walsh and Richard Middleton when they note that, in our times, "truth is stranger than it used to be."[1]

Into such a cultural and philosophical context the Christian church makes a public confession: Jesus Christ is the truth. We have a truth to tell, news that is good, a gospel for all people. The gospel itself commits us to belief in the truth.[2] But what does this mean? What kind of truth is the gospel? Because of the primacy of Scripture in the sources of our knowledge of God in Christ, this question soon becomes: what do we mean when we confess that the Bible is true?

---

1. See J. R. Middleton and B. J. Walsh, *Truth Is Stranger Than It Used to Be: Biblical Faith in a Postmodern Age* (Downers Grove, IL: InterVarsity Press, 1995).

2. One of the strengths of Wolfhart Pannenberg's three-volume *Systematic Theology* is his recognition of the importance of the question of truth for the confession of the gospel. The first chapter of Volume I is "The Truth of Christian Doctrine as a Theme of Systematic Theology" (W. Pannenberg, *Systematic Theology*, Vol. I [Grand Rapids: Eerdmans, 1991], pp. 1-62). We agree on the importance of this question for Christian doctrine, even if we do not approach it the way Pannenberg does.

All of the authors in this volume came to agree on one thing. We all reject a common, too-simple answer to this question, which would reduce truth to true propositions. For those who reduce all truth to true propositions, the Bible is true only because it teaches true propositions — empirical, moral, and religious — concerning God and the world.[3] Associated with this approach in fundamentalism and conservative evangelicalism is an insistence on interpreting the Bible "literally." This viewpoint begins with the false assumption that the only things that can be true are true propositions. Just as language does more than convey information (as the later Wittgenstein argued at length), so also truth is more than true propositions. There is, of course, propositional truth, but is it the only kind? A richer, more nuanced and holistic conception of truth is needed to account for personal disclosure, truth in art, and also religious revelation.[4]

We begin our volume with a meditation on Scripture's own understanding of truth. Dennis Olson provides an extensive reflection on the notion of truth in the Pentateuch, as well as giving us the title for our collective volume. The Hebrew term for truth, 'emet, was the subject of much conversation among our participants, and Olson does a superb job of theological interpretation regarding truth in relationship with the God of the Torah. Among his many interesting conclusions is that, for the Pentateuch, truth is primarily about moving into a deeper relationship with and understanding of God over a long period of time, within the community of God's people.

We next consider more philosophical questions surrounding truth and Scripture. Nicholas Wolterstorff, in his chapter entitled "True Words," draws on several senses of the term "truth" as this is applied to Scripture, concluding that "true" often has the sense of measuring up to some standard in being or excellence.

In the third chapter biblical scholar Ben Ollenburger provides a rich interpretation and response to Wolterstorff's recent book *Divine Discourse*, as well as to his ideas in the second chapter. Ollenburger's response in-

3. For a recent defense of this view, see Carl F. H. Henry, *God, Revelation and Authority*, 6 vols. (Waco, TX: Word Books, 1976-1983), especially 3:429-87.
4. I expand on this point in Chapter 6 of this volume.

volves not only the discipline of biblical studies but also philosophical hermeneutics and his own Mennonite theological tradition. He presses home this question: Is Scripture faithful to God?

The next chapter, by Mark Wallace, approaches the question from a quite different philosophical tradition (continental and postmodern). Wallace sees meaning as created in the dynamic act of reading a text, generated in the living interplay between text and reader. Instead of grounding his understanding of truth in logic and propositions, Wallace connects it more fully to moral goodness. He relates his understanding of the truth of Scripture to larger concerns: what the Bible means in its fullness and integrity as a compelling theological witness addressed to the deepest questions of human life. Wallace enters into dialogue with several participants in the colloquium, including Wolterstorff, Keifert, and Davis. He picks up the Augustinian point that a truly Christian interpretation of Scripture (and its truth) orients the reader toward the love of God and neighbor. Developing a reader-response conception of meaning, Wallace argues that biblical truth is enacted: it is the ethical performance of what the Spirit says to the reader in and through the biblical text. Since God is love, love becomes a central test of truth for any "meaning" we live out of the scriptural text. This means that texts that are dark, violent, and oppressive must be opposed and rejected — not simply submitted to — by the Christian community. The contribution of this chapter is to focus on the interchange between love and Spirit in the dynamic act of reading/enacting Scripture.

The chapter by Stephen Davis, an analytic philosopher and an evangelical theologian, begins with our central question: "What do we mean when we say that the Bible is true?" He notes that simply saying the Bible contains a series of true statements does not get at what orthodox Christians want to say about the Bible. Rather, for Davis, the Bible is true because we believe that God speaks to us in its pages. For that reason, the truth of Scripture implies that we submit ourselves to its teachings. We trust it to guide our lives. We allow our rational structures and beliefs to be influenced by them. In short, we submit ourselves to the theological authority of Scripture. In developing this viewpoint, Davis enters into conversation with two of the other Christian philosophers who contributed to this book, Nicholas Wolterstorff and Mark Wallace.

I propose in my chapter an understanding of truth that is grounded in the Gospel of John's confession of Jesus Christ as the way, the truth, and the life. Rather than using a strict definition, I suggest that we understand truth in a variety of contexts as the mediated disclosure of being (or reality). This makes sense not only of saying that Christ as God in human flesh is the Truth, but also the notion that Scripture is true because it discloses to us the living Word of God, that is, Jesus Christ. This chapter leads into David Bartlett's presentation of "Preaching the Truth." Bartlett also begins with a reflection on truth in the Gospel of John: how do we attend to the question of historical truth (and the critical methods that seek it) when we are preaching the Truth incarnate in Jesus Christ? For the Christian preacher, the shape of truth is defined by Jesus Christ and encountered in the biblical text. Moving deftly among philosophers and theologians, Bartlett argues that the historical reality of Christ and God's people demands that we pay some attention to the history behind the text, as well as to the realities of our own culture, when we preach the truth of Scripture today.

The final two chapters of this book focus on theological education. Patrick Keifert develops a rhetorical approach to theological education, which comes from many years of teaching about the Bible, truth, and meaning with Donald Juel (see also the second part of this introduction). The public interpretation of Scripture in local congregations, and in other Christian practices, is the living context in which we seek to know God truly. It is exactly in this context that one rightly asks about the truth and meaning of Scripture. The truth of the Bible, as an indirect means of knowing God truly, is grounded in the activity of God, who uses these texts to shape and enliven these communities of faith. A key theme of this chapter is promise: God promises through word and sacrament to gather people and finally the whole creation into the blessedness of the Triune life.

From a very different theological perspective, Ellen Charry reflects on what it means to know the truth — and thus to know God. She comes to conclusions that are similar to Keifert's, though she makes her argument in a very different idiom. She calls the church today to return to a theological education that is grounded in the truth of God, understood in personal, relational, and thus spiritual terms. In tracing the historical rise of theological studies, she attributes the loss of a sapiential theological approach, and the attendant rise of scholastic theology, to the founding of universities in Europe. This rationalist approach to theology was strengthened during the Enlightenment period, leading to an objectification of truth and a rationalist, academic theology. Charry makes the case that seeking the truth of God today requires a return to the affective, sapiential, and spiritual dimension of knowing God.

A.G.P.

Easter 2005

II. Scripture, Truth, and Rhetoric: Shared Theological Labors

For over twenty years, my good friend and colleague Donald H. Juel and I reflected together on the place of the Bible in modern theological education. This second part of the introduction to this book sketches why we set out together on that journey, so that others might come to make their own; it also offers some brief reflections about why these travels are so necessary, not only for the life of the church but for the flourishing of our postmodern world. Further discussion of these themes is found in my contribution (Chapter 8) to this volume.

Though we found a plenitude of ways to describe what we were trying to learn, one question — in two parts — serves to capture our inquiry: When we say the Bible is true, what do we mean? And what methods of interpretation appreciate its truthfulness? We came to this question as we explored two locations where the Bible is commonly thought to be central, indeed critical, to theological discourse: the academy, especially theological institutions and departments of religion, and the Christian congregation. As we ventured out for answers, we began by reflecting on how various centers of learning within the academy understand the Bible as true, and what methods of interpretation they use to appreciate its truthfulness. We were curious not only about how particular methods of interpretation and application were justified, but also how those methods actually are used in practical situations by those who espouse them. As time went on and the significant conflict among scholars and disciplines on these questions became more apparent, we became more and more interested in how our colleagues in the academy actually persuaded each other to change their minds regarding these questions.

As another part of our journey, we focused on how people encountered the Bible in moral conversations in the congregations, and particularly how scholars, teachers, and congregational leaders used the Bible to convince those diverse audiences of a moral or interpretive position. The congregational practices we found were, in a few instances, quite encouraging; but more often than not, what we saw was discouraging.

The realities of these practices in both the academy and church caused us to re-examine the use of the Bible in theological education. To begin with, we found that our own previous academic training was, at least in part, disturbingly inadequate in preparing us to pursue these questions of truth, and that various individuals and structures within the academy employed practices of critique and persuasion that were equally inadequate. Our academic training had caused us to wonder about the relationship between traditional claims that the Bible is true and the methods we used and taught for interpreting the Bible. For us, as with other modern students of the Bible, history was the primary "mode of intelligibility,"[5] the key methodology we had learned for understanding the truth claims of the Bible. However, we joined many students of the Bible who have found that such a method has led to an unhappy and dysfunctional divide between what we, following Martin Buss, have called "critical description and capricious faith,"[6] that is, between empirical or rationalist

---

5. "History as a mode of intelligibility" came into my vocabulary in a class by the same title at Chicago taught by Charles Wegener; see his *Liberal Education and the Modern University* (Chicago: University of Chicago Press, 1978), and *The Discipline of Taste and Feeling* (Chicago: University of Chicago Press, 1992).

6. Martin J. Buss, ed., *Encounter with the Text: Form and History in the Hebrew Bible* (Philadelphia: Fortress, 1979), p. 5. Describing a quite different phenomenon, twentieth-century literature on parents, Stacy Schiff notes a pattern of either "scientific or sermonic" discourse with little in between (*The New York Times Book Review*, April 27, 2003, 9).

engagement with the text as a historical document and nonrational commitments to the Bible as the word of God. This complete separation between two approaches to the role of the Bible — critical description and capricious faith — proved to be present in the thought and practice of the academy as well as the congregation. Indeed, the divide was especially noticeable in conversations and decisions of Christian congregations on morally controversial issues.[7]

As we reflected on the set of problems associated with the use of the Bible in our own scholarship and teaching, and in the practices of congregational leaders, Donald and I found strong consonance between the disturbing patterns we were witnessing and the analysis of several scholars who have called for a postmodern retrieval of the ancient rhetorical tradition to shape secular public discourse. Donald joined me in studying how the work of three of my teachers at the University of Chicago — Wayne C. Booth, Stephen Toulmin, and Paul Ricoeur (who had informed my early itinerary of reflection on rhetorical approaches) — might teach the church about its own conversations.

Even though they represent three different strains of Western philosophy, these scholars concur in rather significant ways with the analysis of this problematic on the use of the Bible and on the promise of the rhetorical approach in responding to it. Our conversation with these three thinkers deepened our analysis and funded our growing sense that a rhetorical approach to theological education in general, and especially for using the Bible in that setting, held some hope for the church.

Perhaps Booth's early work *The Modern Dogma and the Rhetoric of Assent* clarified our initial diagnosis of the situation best.[8] This volume, which presents in published form lectures he delivered to undergraduates of the University of Notre Dame in the spring of 1970, reflects the realities of that turbulent time in American society. Then dean at the University of Chicago, Booth had been granted leave by student protesters, who had placed

---

7. These findings are described in greater length in Patrick R. Keifert, "The Bible, Congregational Leaders, and Moral Conversation," in *Word and World* 13/4 (1993): 392-97.

8. *The Modern Dogma and the Rhetoric of Assent* (Notre Dame, IN: University of Notre Dame Press, 1974).

him under "house arrest" in the University's administration building, to travel and deliver the lectures at Notre Dame.

Nevertheless, Booth's telling lectures about the collapse of public discourse on the college campuses found less fault with the students and more with the failure of his colleagues in the elite circles of the academy. In Booth's view, the latter had failed to engage in sustained reflection with one another on the questions of the day because they uncritically accepted a set of deep assumptions about the relationship of truth-seeking and the good of the community in public conversation. He called this dysfunctional set of assumptions the "modern dogma." These assumptions revealed a deep divide in modernity, built around the fact/value split. Booth's analysis exactly fit the patterns we found in the use of the Bible within the academy and the church: that is, they displayed a vast gulf between the activities of "critical description" and "capricious faith."

In response to the fact/value split, Booth called for a "rhetoric of assent," his own retrieval of the premodern practice of rhetoric. The rhetoric of assent is intended to move the essence of critical intellectual inquiry beyond the practices of systemic doubt established by Descartes and Hume. Taking aim directly at the thought and life of one of the reigning philosophers of the twentieth century, Bertrand Russell, Booth demonstrates how the latter's adoption of the rhetoric of systemic doubt and the other contours of the modern dogma led him to incoherence, immorality, and failed leadership as a public intellectual.

Stephen Toulmin, a student of Ludwig Wittgenstein, had already developed his own itinerary for what, in his most popular work, *Cosmopolis*,[9] he terms "rhetorical rationality." Toulmin had explored modern human understanding and discovered some of the same patterns at which Booth had taken aim. However, Toulmin deepened Booth's analysis and response to the modern condition by exploring, in ever wider and deeper circles, the historical and cultural developments that brought about the modern dogma[10] and effective ways of arguing or engaging in discourse

---

9. *Cosmopolis: The Hidden Agenda of Modernity* (Boston: Free Press, 1990).

10. Stephen Toulmin, *Return to Reason* (Cambridge, MA: Harvard University Press, 2001).

that made possible sustained public understanding and truth seeking.[11] His exploration of the use of the practical syllogism[12] and the ancient tradition of casuistry[13] has profoundly influenced our exploration of the place of the Bible in both the academy and the church.

Most importantly, Paul Ricoeur's phenomenology of the will, used within the framework of a rhetorical rationality,[14] has shaped our understanding of the actual interpretation of the Bible in academy and church, funding our sustained work toward developing new theories of interpretation and truth. Ricoeur's dedication to engaging the greatest *aporia* of modernity and, at the same time, investigating common practices of biblical interpretation, an investigation that he undertook with great patience, subtlety, and complexity, has made such innovation possible.

Donald Juel's own work on the Gospel according to Mark became a shared task in our invention of new theories of interpretation and the truth of the Bible. Beginning with his dissertation, *Messiah and Temple*,[15] he had sought to move beyond the impulse of the historical-critical method to dissect the text in order to seek its truth. Initially, he sought to understand the whole of Mark using the then-adventurous redaction criticism, especially the work of Willi Marxsen.[16] At the same time, he wanted to engage his teacher Nils Dahl's historical work on the crucifixion.[17] In terms

---

11. Stephen Toulmin, Richard Rieke, and Allan Janik, *An Introduction to Reasoning* (New York, 1979).

12. Stephen Toulmin, *The Uses of Argument* (Cambridge, UK: Cambridge University Press, 1958).

13. Albert R. Jonsen and Stephen Toulmin, *The Abuse of Casuistry: A History of Moral Reasoning* (Berkeley, CA: University of California Press, 1988).

14. Ricoeur and Toulmin offered a seminar in which each took his own tradition of thought (Continental and Anglo-American) and reflected on common topics, e.g., practice and action.

15. Donald H. Juel, *Messiah and Temple: The Trial of Jesus in the Gospel of Mark*, SBLDS 31 (Missoula, MT: Scholars Press, 1977).

16. Willi Marxsen, *Mark the Evangelist: Studies on the Redaction History of the Gospel According to Mark*, trans. Donald H. Juel, (and his seminary classmates) James Boyce, William Poehlmann, (and their teacher) Roy A. Harrisville (Nashville: Abingdon, 1969).

17. Nils Alstrup Dahl, *Crucified Messiah and Other Essays*, ed. Donald H. Juel (Minneapolis: Augsburg, 1974).

of our joint work, he often said that he sought to understand the book of Mark as a whole without losing its historical referentiality.[18]

In seeking to keep together our engagement with both the Bible as a whole and its referentiality, we sought to move beyond the fact/value split, especially beyond the modern habit of reducing truth to historical fact, a move that relegates theological meaning and significance to the category of a capricious enterprise.[19]

Ricoeur's careful phenomenology of time and narrative furthered this enterprise.[20] His many-faceted descriptive phenomenology made visible the interaction of plot, narrative, and diverse forms of temporality that uncovered the rhetorical character of historical consciousness. The space between fact and value, once considered by modern scholars an infinite crevasse, becomes in his analysis a multifaceted set of relationships, rendering the split obsolete — indeed silly. In place of reductive schemes of referentiality, we began to see multiple referentiality and polyvalence as the most intellectually persuasive and morally adequate approach to the interpretation of the Bible in the academy and the church as a whole. The use of a rhetorical rationality helped us move, in Richard Bernstein's terms, "beyond objectivism and relativism" and established a rich intellectual and teaching agenda.[21]

The congregational or intellectual leader's capacity to innovate in using rhetorical rationality with the Bible in public discourse must be shaped first by developing seminarians' practices in using the Bible in classes that

18. My own dissertation had argued that a relatively adequate theory of interpretation understood the text as a whole without losing a full range of referentiality. Of course, part of this full range included historical references (Keifert, "Meaning and Reference: The Interpretation of Verisimilitude in the Gospel According to Mark" (Ph.D. dissertation, University of Chicago, 1982).

19. One cannot here use the phrase "meaning and significance" in relationship to this time period without recognizing that this desire was directed at the work of Eric Donald Hirsch, Jr., in *Validity in Interpretation* (New Haven: Yale University Press, 1967) and *The Aims of Interpretation* (Chicago: University of Chicago Press, 1976).

20. Paul Ricoeur, *Time and Narrative*, 3 vols. (Chicago: University of Chicago Press, 1984, 1985, 1988).

21. Richard Bernstein, *Beyond Objectivism and Relativism: Science, Hermeneutics and Praxis* (Philadelphia: University of Pennsylvania Press, 1983).

focus on other subject matters besides the Bible itself. We believed that the paradigm for the use of the Bible in classes could be changed by way of two major shifts in the way we approached the Bible: first, providing students and faculty with practice using the Bible to provide rhetorical warrants and backing for their positions, not just data in a practical syllogism; and second, reshaping our practice of inquiry to consider God as first and always an agent, not simply a subject matter, in the educational process.[22]

This two-fold shift led us to teaching interdisciplinary courses that focused on different subject matters but always attended to using the Bible in the work of the class. However, we wanted to explore this intellectual and teaching agenda in the real world of theological education as a whole. So we wrote a proposal to Craig Dykstra[23] at the Lilly Endowment, which led to a grant to Luther Seminary. Along with our colleague in the field of practical theology, Roland Martinson, we functioned as the research-and-development team for the creation of a curriculum that took this double-premised rhetorical approach to the engagement with the Bible in theological education quite seriously.

When Donald Juel moved to Princeton, our project and our conversation partners broadened and became more diverse. With the generous assistance of the Lilly Endowment, we were able to involve a number of colleagues from other schools of theology in a conversation and critique of our rhetorical approach. This conversation over the last decade has involved scholars, administrators, and teachers from all the disciplines within contemporary schools of theology. The conversation, which has continued under the name "The Bible and Theological Education," has been furthered by the conversations of a steering committee[24] and three

---

22. Eberhard Jüngel, *God as the Mystery of the World* (Grand Rapids: Eerdmans, 1983); see also David Kelsey, *To Understand God Truly: What's Theological about a Theological School* (Louisville: Westminster, 1992) and *Between Athens and Berlin: The Theological Education Debate* (Grand Rapids: Eerdmans, 1993).

23. Our debt to Craig Dykstra and James Wind and the Lilly Endowment goes well beyond the Endowment's financial support to include their genuine interest, engagement, critique, and trust in our enterprise.

24. David L. Bartlett, Beverly Roberts Gaventa, Richard B. Hays, Stephen J. Kraftchick, Dennis T. Olson, Alan Padgett, Donald Juel, and Patrick Keifert.

project teams. The first team, whose initial study volume was completed first, explored the nature of the study of theology within the rubric of rhetorical rationality.[25] This work has uncovered the profoundly important role of rhetorical rationality in the preparation and practices of Christian leaders in the first four centuries of the church.[26] Indeed, these researchers have concluded that, unless we view their work with an understanding of rhetorical practice, our understanding of their vision and practices is greatly flattened and diminished. This team also examined how moral and doctrinal questions have been examined throughout the history of the church, using a rhetorical approach. Among other things, we have learned how profound are the differences in how we now understand the basic teachings of the Trinity when we start with a rhetorical approach.[27]

A second team in this conversation has focused on the use of the rhetorical approach within the classroom.[28] Interdisciplinary teams of faculty have attempted to rethink their classes using a rhetorical imagination, considering how rhetorical rationality might affect the structure of the curriculum as a whole (as well as the character of the classroom itself), and outlining how they might use learning activities appropriate to teach these necessary capacities of Christian leadership. Much of the group's time has been spent reviewing these proposed courses created by teams from the various schools of theology.[29]

---

25. A. K. M. Adam, Wesley Avram, James Boyce, Donald Compiers, David W. Cunningham, Susan K. Heydahl, Frederick W. Norris, Richard R. Osmer, Janet Weathers, Stephen H. Webb, Donald Juel, and Patrick Keifert.

26. Frederick Norris, "Nazianzus," in *To Teach, to Delight and to Move: Theological Education in a Postmodern World*, ed. David Cunningham (Eugene, OR: Cascade Books, 2005); also, with Lionel Wickham and Frederick Williams, *Faith Gives Fullness to Reasoning: The Five Theological Orations of Gregory of Nasiansen*, Vigiliae Christianae, Supplements, 13 (Leiden: E. J. Brill, 1991).

27. Ibid.

28. A. K. M. Adam, James Boyce, Ellen T. Charry, Sarah Henrichs, Stephen J. Kraftchick, Dennis T. Olson, Marianne Meye Thompson, John Thompson, and Miroslav Volf.

29. Perkins School of Theology, Azusa Pacific University, Candler School of Theology, Duke Divinity, Yale Divinity, Princeton Theological Seminary, Fuller Seminary, St. Paul Seminary at the University of St. Thomas, Lutheran Schools of Theology in Chicago, Philadelphia, and Gettysburg, and Luther Seminary.

Within the conversation that we have sustained about the Bible and theological education, we have encountered both surface concerns and deeper doubts and questions about the limits of rhetorical rationality and the potential flaws in a rhetorical approach to theological education. The third team in the "Bible and Theological Education" project, long anticipated but only recently formed in this decade-long project, is composed of philosophers, theologians, and Bible scholars who want to respond to both ancient and modern suspicions that rhetoric is too often used as a way to avoid or confuse questions of truth.[30]

In public life we often hear the expression "mere rhetoric." Those who use it do so with some suspicion that their audience is being manipulated rather than convinced. Their use of the term suggests that, to them, rhetoric refers to the means of communication, the outward form rather than the inner substance of a message. Or again, we commonly refer to "rhetorical questions" as questions to which the answer is already assumed — questions that need no discussion. Though this is not what we mean by rhetoric, this common usage of the word "rhetorical" captures something at the core of proposals for rhetorical rationality: namely, rhetoric actually pays attention to the audience and what the people assume to be the case in the world in which they live.

Aristotle notes that all speeches reveal three characters: the character of the speaker (ethos), the character of the speech (logos), and the character of the audience (pathos).[31] Thus, rhetorical rationality understands that all discourse takes place within a particular setting, that it is aimed at a particular audience, and that it is delivered by particular speakers who use assumed warrants and backing for their claims within a moral field.[32] It's

---

30. David Bartlett, Ellen Charry, Stephen Davis, Dennis Olson, Alan Padgett, Marianne Meye Thompson, Mark Wallace, Nicholas Wolterstorff, Donald Juel, and Patrick Keifert.

31. Aristotle, *The Rhetoric*, 2:1.

32. Stephen Toulmin's layout of an argument consists of six elements: (1) the claim: the claim of the argument is the conclusion that someone is trying to justify in the argument; (2) the grounds: the grounds of an argument are the facts on which the argument is based; (3) the warrant: the warrant of the argument assesses whether or not the claim is legitimate based on the grounds; (4) the backing: the backing of the argument gives additional support for a warrant by answering different questions; (5) the modal qualifier: the modal qualifier

about character. We might say that it is this moral embeddedness of all discourse, indeed of all knowledge, in implicit values or human interests of particular times and places that much of the intellectual project of modernity has sought to escape.[33]

With these issues well in mind, the "Truth and the Bible" team went to work.[34] The team deliberately put philosophers, theologians, and biblical scholars together with the express purpose of exploring the question of truth from the point of view of these philosophical questions in such a way that they could serve our goal of deepening the study and use of the Bible in classrooms and in local congregations. The result of this collaborative conversation is the excellent collaborative work that now lies before you.

Despite their diverse perspectives on what constitutes the most adequate theories of truth, all members of this team have participated in the study of the Bible and reflected on their proposals in light of their actual reading of the Bible. Philosophers and theologians have sought to interpret the Bible, both in the presence of biblical scholars and also in partnership with these scholars, in the service of the use of the Bible in classroom and congregation. Donald Juel was a valuable ally to all involved in this quest. He inculcated the habits and virtues of model biblical scholarship and Christian discipleship. Donald was always inviting others to join him in the quest for truth, meaning, and a deeper faith in Christ. He was especially inviting to his students. All of us involved in this project remember with joy his energy, humor, and playfulness. We dedicate this collection to his memory, in gratitude to the God who brings such servants into our midst; and who saves us through the Son, who is the way, the truth, and the life everlasting.

P.R.K.

Easter 2005

---

indicates the strength of the leap from the data to the warrant; (6) the rebuttal: the rebuttal occurs when the leap from grounds to claim does not appear to be legitimate.

33. Jürgen Habermas, *Knowledge and Human Interests*, trans. Jeremy J. Shapiro (Boston: Beacon Press, 1971); Toulmin, *Return to Reason*, pp. 67-82.

34. Alan Padgett, Marianne Meye Thompson, Stephen Davis, Nicholas Wolterstorff, Mark Wallace, David Bartlett, Patrick Keifert, Donald Juel, Ellen Charry, and Michael Welker.

Truth and the Torah: Reflections on Rationality and the Pentateuch

DENNIS T. OLSON

Several summers ago I was sitting at home at our kitchen table reading a *Time* magazine article about the end of the universe.[1] Scientists agree that our universe is expanding. Tens of billions of galaxies, each containing hundreds of billions of stars, are all rushing headlong away from each other in the aftermath of the cosmic Big Bang, which occurred some fifteen billion years ago. But scientists have disagreed about how all of this will end. Will the galaxies continue to fly apart forever? Will the glow and heat of stars and planets just gradually fade away until the cosmos grows cold and dark — with all matter disintegrating into molecule-sized particles? Or will the expansion of the universe slow to a halt, reverse direction under the pull of the combined gravity of all those galaxies and stars, and then eventually send those billions of galaxies crashing back together in a final, super-heated, apocalyptic "Big Crunch"? Scientists subscribing to the Big Crunch theory like to quote the poet Robert Frost: "Some say the world will end in fire,/Some say in ice./From what I have tasted of desire/I hold with those who favor fire." On the other hand, scientists who believe the universe will exit in a slow, cold disintegrative fade prefer the words of T. S. Eliot: "This is the way the world ends/Not with a bang but a whimper."

In light of recent discoveries, the *Time* article concluded that T. S. Eliot

---

1. "The End of the Universe," *Time*, June 25, 2001, pp. 48-56.

was probably closer to the truth: the universe will end in a cold, icy whimper, but not until another ten thousand trillion trillion trillion trillion trillion trillion trillion years have passed. The article notes that humans will be long gone by then; they will have survived for at most one or two billion more years, as our sun slowly heats up and eventually boils off the earth's oceans. So, perhaps from the context and perspective of most interest to us as humans in our small solar system, Frost had it right after all: "I hold with those who favor fire."

As I sat at the kitchen table, Kristen, my 18-year-old daughter, breezed by and asked cheerily, "So what are you reading about, Dad?" Now you need to know that there is a history between my daughter and me. She is our doubting Thomas, our Qoheleth who questions all conventional wisdom, our faithful prodigal who cries, "Lord, I believe; help my unbelief!" She and I have had many long dialogues about God, life, love, and the meaning of it all. So I told her that I was reading scientific views concerning the end of the universe. Predictably, she took the bait. She stopped in her tracks, her eyes brightened, and she slid into a nearby chair. Suddenly we were into one of our talks about life, death, and God. "Life is so weird," she said. "People live, they work hard, and then they just die. You're buried or cremated or whatever, and then you're supposed to go to heaven. What does that mean? Is it all true?" We talked a long time about weighty matters, probing the meaning of the end of the universe and the end of life. She told me the next day that she had introduced the topic to a group of her friends later that same evening, which had engendered, in her words "a great discussion." She added with a wry smile, "You know, Dad, I really enjoy our big, deep conversations." One of the unique attributes of the human animal is this wondrous capacity and passion for big, deep conversations, its ability consciously to reflect on itself and the world, on truth and the meaning of it all.

In what many have called our postmodern context, this human yearning and quest for truth and knowledge about God, humans, and the universe has been seriously threatened and eroded. Seminary professors often hear the laments of students dazed and bewildered by today's multiplicity of perspectives in the disciplines of philosophy, theology, sociology, history, the sciences, and the study of the Bible. What is truth, and how do we live it out? What understanding of God is the true one? What reading of a biblical text, or what construal of the whole Christian thing, is true? And how do we arrive at such a conclusion? These questions echo the plaintive lament of an elderly and impatient Abraham, a man yearning for the fulfillment of God's promises in Genesis 15: "Oh LORD God, how am I to know?" (Gen. 15:8).

The "big, deep conversations" about truth are often lodged in the disciplines of philosophy and theology. In a time such as ours, when the debates about the nature of truth are in some turmoil, it is important for biblical scholars to be attentive to these conversations. I have noticed a tendency in some of these discussions to relegate the Bible to the role of a voiceless object for investigation rather than a genuine partner in the conversation. In this chapter I argue that Scripture itself, as a rich and complex canon of interpreted experience, offers to us important insights into the nature of truth and truth-seeking about God, ourselves, and the world. For the purposes of this book, I confine myself to five insights into the nature of truth and truth-seeking that emerge from reflections on the Pentateuch, or Torah, the first five books of Hebrew Scripture (the Old Testament) — Genesis through Deuteronomy.

1. Postmodern challenges in religious truth-seeking (a hermeneutics of suspicion, deconstruction, pluralism, and the like) have seeds at least as old as the garden of Eden and the tower of Babel.

The crafty serpent in the garden of Eden in Genesis 3 is the first biblical character to apply a hermeneutics of suspicion to the word of God. In Genesis 2, God had commanded the human: "You may freely eat of every tree of the garden; but of the tree of the knowledge of good and evil you shall not eat, for in the day that you eat of it you shall surely die" (Gen. 2:16-17). But the serpent convinces the woman that this command from God is an ideological lie. The "real" truth, says the serpent, is this: "You will not die; for God knows that when you eat of it, your eyes will be opened, and you will be like God, knowing good and evil" (Gen. 3:4-5). In other words, the serpent claims that God just wants to keep the humans ignorant and less than God. If they eat the fruit, they will become God's equal. The humans will not die because God will not be able to destroy them. However, the serpent's words obfuscate and mix truth and falsehood. Yes, it is true, the humans do not die on the day they eat the fruit; the serpent is correct on that score. But the rest of the biblical story makes clear that the reason the humans do not die is not God's weakness. God had the power to destroy the whole human experiment all along, which the flood story in Genesis 6–9 makes clear. The reason God allows the humans to live is God's continuing commitment to and compassion for humans in spite of their disobedience.

The entire story of Adam and Eve's rebellion in the garden of Eden swirls around issues of truth: knowing the truth, skewing the truth, hiding the truth, and dodging the truth. From Eden on, human truth-seeking would be flawed and corrupt, entwined with secrecy and shame, suspicion and envy, power and violence. Thus we find Cain's murder of Abel in Genesis 4, and then the interplay of corrupted truth and worldwide violence at the beginning of the flood story in Genesis 6: "The LORD saw that . . . every inclination of the thoughts of their hearts was only evil continually. . . . The earth was corrupt in God's sight, and the earth was filled with violence" (Gen. 6:5, 11).

The pluralism of languages and the challenges of communicating truth are implicit in the story of the tower of Babel in Genesis 11:1-9. The narrative begins in a primeval time, when "the whole earth had one language and the same words." This unified global community builds a city and a tower on the model of a Babylonian ziggurat, a tall pyramid-like structure that Mesopotamian priests ascended to communicate with the gods in the heavens. The construction of the tall tower is motivated by a human fear of fragmentation and chaos: "Otherwise we shall be scattered abroad upon the face of the whole earth" (Gen. 11:4). God discerns that the heaven-storming tower built by humans in order to make a name for themselves is just the first of untold horrors that the worldwide church of human potential may construct for itself. Thus God scatters the human community into its various nations and cultures across the earth and confuses their language. From Babel onward humans will be inextricably caught in webs of conflicting perspectives and counterbalancing powers. Communication across boundaries of culture, time, and language will be difficult and restricted. Such pluralism is God's strategy for limiting the damage humans can do to themselves. We seek truth within the realities of a God-given pluralism of perspectives and languages. It is a pluralism that will not soon go away.

2. The primary Hebrew noun for "truth" (*'emet*; אמת) in the Pentateuch signifies both relational trust as well as a more objective testing for truth.

The Old Testament word for "truth" has as its root the three-consonant Hebrew verb *'mn* אמנ, "to be reliable, sure, firm, enduring, trustworthy," and in the causative *Hiphil* stem, "to stand firm, to trust, believe in." The object of the trust is typically a person, a message, or a promise. The root is related to the word we often append to the end of our prayers to God, "Amen," which affirms the truth of what we pray and the trust we have in the One to whom we address the prayer. We can make three observations about the use of the word *'emet* in Genesis-Deuteronomy:

a. In five of its eleven occurrences in the Pentateuch, *'emet* ("truth, faithfulness") is paired with the word *hesed*, "steadfast love, enduring loyalty." This fixed word pair of "steadfast love and faithfulness" is used to describe both human-to-human relationships (three times) and the divine-to-human relationship (twice). In the dramatic and definitive self-revelation of God's character to Moses on Mount Sinai, the LORD proclaims, "The LORD, the LORD, a God merciful and gracious, slow to anger, and abounding in steadfast love [*hesed*] and faithfulness [*'emet*]" (Exod. 34:6). Truth here involves a character of reliability and trustworthiness in relationships over time, grounded in past experience and extending in confidence into an as yet unseen future.

b. Five other occurrences of the word *'emet* have to do with determining truth as a more objective fact-finding through evidence and testing, particularly in legal investigations involving the determination of guilt and innocence. In Deuteronomy, diligent inquiry is required in order to test the reliability of hearsay evidence and to determine "if it be true [*'emet*] and established [*nakôn*] that such an abhorrent thing has been done among you" (Deut. 13:14; 17:4; see also Deut. 22:20). Material evidence and the testimony of witnesses provide grounds for determining the truth (or *'emet*) of a matter.

c. One other use of the word *'emet* combines the two senses of personal trustworthiness and the more objective seeking of truth based on evidence and testimony. In Exodus 18, the Midianite Jethro instructs his son-in-law Moses to share the heavy burden of adjudicating disputes within the community by appointing a number of additional judges who will serve alongside Moses. Jethro enumerates the qualities that such judges should possess: "Look for able men from all the people, men who fear God, men of truth ['emet] who hate bribes" (Exod. 18:21). Here truth and the character of trustworthiness are linked with fearing God and hating bribes. Moses adopts this Midianite wisdom coming from outside Israel, and he incorporates it later in his final words of teaching to a new generation of Israelites in the book of Deuteronomy. In the section of Deuteronomy's laws concerning the appointment of judges, Moses issues these instructions to the judges and provides us with some insight into Israel's understanding of truth and its relationship to justice:

> You must not distort justice; you must not show partiality; and you must not accept bribes, for a bribe blinds the eyes of the wise and subverts the cause of those who are in the right. Justice, and only justice, you shall pursue (Deut. 16:19-20; see also Exod. 23:8).

Our modern Western assumption about judges is that one of their primary roles is to apply the rules or laws that the legislating body of the nation or community has established to a given case, even though such application sometimes involves considerable interpretation and adaptation. Bernard Jackson has argued that this modern Western model of judges is somewhat different in emphasis from the one presupposed in ancient Israel. Jackson writes:

> The judges are here [in Deuteronomy] told simply to act justly and avoid corruption. They are not asked to follow any particular rules. I am not, of course, suggesting that they are being given an entirely free discretion. The passage has clear wisdom connections, as seen by the proverb used as a motive clause ["for a bribe blinds the eyes of the wise and subverts the cause of those who are in the right" — v. 19]. That seems to me to be a clue as to the kind of criteria which the judge is ex-

pected to apply: his sense of justice is to be tempered by the conventional norms of practical wisdom.[2]

According to Deuteronomy, the primary role of Israelite judges was not to apply laws to specific cases and let the chips fall where they may. Rather, the judges sought to negotiate and arbitrate disputes and so work toward a consensus of the community. In communities structured by kinship and tribal forms of alliances as in ancient Israel,[3] the primary goal of judges and their truth-seeking was the restoration of the community and the relationships involved in the dispute.[4] Judges were selected because they were respected as "wise, discerning and reputable" (Deut. 1:13). Part of truth-seeking involved a rhetorical transaction of trust between actual judges and a real-life community — leaders and followers, experts and lay people. Such truth-seeking is as much about building trust and restoring community relationships as it is about finding and knowing "the facts."

At the same time, these instructions to judges affirm the need to strive for some sense of objectivity and impartiality. "You must not distort justice; you must not show partiality; and you must not accept bribes" (Deut. 16:19). Michael Goldberg has argued that this prohibition of bribes is a somewhat distinctive element compared to other ancient Near Eastern conceptions of judges.[5] The practice of offering a gift or bribe to the judge in order for a verdict to be rendered in one's favor was a known and some-

---

2. Bernard Jackson, "Legalism and Spirituality," in *Religion and Law, Judaic and Islamic Perspectives*, ed. Edwin Firmage et al. (Winona Lake: Eisenbraun, 1990), p. 245.

3. Kinship and tribal structures remained important in ancient Israel, even during and after the time of the Israelite monarchy. Cf. Timothy Willis, *The Elders of the City: A Study of Elders-Laws in Deuteronomy*, SBL Monograph Series, ed. Dennis T. Olson (Atlanta: Society of Biblical Literature, 2001).

4. Robert R. Wilson, "Israel's Judicial System in the Pre-Exilic Period," *Jewish Quarterly Review* 74 (1983): 229-48, esp. 235-40; and Moshe Weinfeld, "Judge and Officer in Ancient Israel and the Ancient Near East," *Israel Oriental Society* 7 (1977): 67-76.

5. Michael Goldberg, "The Story of the Moral: Gifts or Bribes in Deuteronomy," *Interpretation* 38 (1984): 15-25. Goldberg cites several Near Eastern examples of judges expecting bribes or gifts. Even some of the wisdom sayings in the book of Proverbs assume this Near Eastern practice of giving gifts as bribes for favorable treatment (Prov. 17:18; 21:14; cf. also 2 Chron. 19:6-7).

times accepted practice in some cultures of the ancient Near East. Goldberg traces the reason for Israel's strict prohibition of bribes in court cases to Israel's conception of God. The prohibition of bribes to judges had a theological reason: Deuteronomy 10:17-18 affirms that "the LORD your God is God of gods and Lord of lords, the great God, mighty and awesome, who is not partial and takes no bribe, who executes justice for the orphan and the widow, and who loves the strangers, providing them food and clothing." This affirmation occurs in the context of God's election of Israel as God's own people, an election founded on God's spontaneous and un-motivated love for Israel. Israel brought no bribe or gift to the table, such as superior strength, material possessions, or moral righteousness to moti-vate God's election.[6] Thus the good human judge of truth in the Old Testa-ment holds in tension two dimensions of truth (or *'emet*): testing truth with some measure of attempted objectivity and impartiality balanced by prac-tical wisdom and striving for reconciliation within the rhetorical context of a real-life community of trusting relationships.

The tests for distinguishing true and false prophecy in the Pentateuch have a similar dual dimension. On the one hand, true prophecy must demonstrate some degree of an objective (if not always precise) corre-spondence between the prophet's predictions and what actually happens "out there" in the real world of history.[7] The law concerning true and false prophets in Deuteronomy 18:21-22 says:

6. Dennis T. Olson, *Deuteronomy and the Death of Moses: A Theological Reading*, Overtures to Biblical Theology (Minneapolis: Fortress, 1994), pp. 52-58.

7. Compare John Barton, "History and Rhetoric in the Prophets," in *The Bible as Rhetoric: Studies in Biblical Persuasion and Credibility*, ed. Martin Warner (London: Routledge, 1990), pp. 51-64; Benjamin Sommer, *A Prophet Reads Scripture: Allusion in Isaiah 40–66* (Stanford, CA: Stanford University Press, 1998); and David Lyle Jeffrey, "How to Read the Hebrew Prophets," in *Mappings of the Biblical Terrain: The Bible as Text*, ed. Vincent Tollers and John Maier (Cranbury, NJ: Associated University Presses, 1990). Sommers and Jeffrey note how the prophets interpret present and future historical events in light of patterns discerned in earlier traditions, both prophetic and Pentateuchal. Barton argues that the writers and edi-tors of the prophetic books used some interpretive license in shaping their descriptions of historical events to fit their message. There was not always an absolute one-to-one corre-spondence of prophecies and external events. Prophetic oracles underwent a process of se-lecting, editing, shaping, and reinterpreting in light of new historical events.

You may say to yourself, "How can we recognize a word that the LORD has not spoken?" [Answer:] If a prophet speaks in the name of the LORD but the thing does not take place or prove true, it is a word that the LORD has not spoken.

But if the event did happen as the prophet said it would, that would be some evidence that he or she may be a true prophet. Thus, for example, the historical report of the actual events of Babylon's capture of Jerusalem in 587 B.C.E. and the exile of the people of Judah recorded in 2 Kings 24–25 is copied from the narrative of 2 Kings and attached to the end of the prophetic oracles in the book of Jeremiah (Jer. 52). The historical report of the exile verifies that Jeremiah with his oracles of judgment against Judah was indeed a true prophet. What he predicted came true.

On the other hand, there is a second and even more important criterion for a true prophet: the prophet must demonstrate and encourage loyalty and love for the LORD alone rather than any foreign gods. Loyalty to God, integrity, and trust are important criteria for who speaks the truth — along with a degree of correspondence to a perceived external reality (Deut. 13:1-5).

3. Humans in the Pentateuch are given only partial glimpses of God and the truth of God's promises.

In matters of truth about God and God's promises, humans receive genuine but partial glimpses, fleeting encounters, and provisional signs of some larger truth or future fulfillment. Abraham cried to God, "Oh LORD God, how am I to know?" (Gen. 15:8). God answered Abraham's question with repeated verbal assurances that Abraham would become a great nation with innumerable descendants who would have a land to call their own (Gen. 12:1-3; 17:15-22; 18:10). Abraham had a vision in which God laid God's very life on the line in a mysterious covenant ceremony, in which the fiery torch of God's presence passed through the middle of split animal carcasses, a pledge that God would keep the promise or else become split in two like the halved animals (Gen. 15:7-11, 17-21; cf. Jer. 34:18-20). Every evening Abraham could see in the stars of the heavens God's promise of the number of his descendants. He saw with his own eyes the wide expanse of Canaan, the land God promised that his descendants would inherit (Gen. 13:14-18). These were all glimpses of a promise yet to be fulfilled. In the end, Abraham held with his century-old hands the promised child, Isaac, the one tangible link to God's promised future (Gen. 21:1-3). At the end of his life, Abraham purchased a modest plot of land for an exorbitant price as a burial plot for Sarah. The cemetery was a small but real down payment on the whole land of Canaan that eventually would be given to his descendants (Gen. 23:1-20).

When God calls Moses to lead the Israelites out of their slavery in Egypt in Exodus 3–4, Moses offers five objections to accepting this call. One of Moses' objections is this: "But suppose [the Israelites] do not believe me or listen to me, but say, 'The LORD did not appear to you.'" God responds to Moses' concern by giving him three "signs" or wonders that will convince the people: Moses will be able to change his staff into a live serpent; he will be able to make his hand leprous and then instantly heal it; and he will be able to change the water of the Nile River into blood (Exod. 4:1-9). These are glimpses, or foreshadowings, of God's much greater power that will work through Moses as he will eventually lead Israel out of Egypt and defeat Pharaoh and his army.

Although Moses is led to a uniquely profound and intimate knowledge of God that surpasses that of all other humans,[8] still he is allowed to see only the back side of the form of God (Exod. 33:20-23). Moses does not and cannot see the full face of God. The image is a metaphor for the hidden and incomprehensible side of God, which no human can know.[9] There will always be some mystery in understanding God's character. But there will also be enough truth so that trust and obedience to God can be passed on to the next generation. As Moses tells the new generation in Deuteronomy 29:29: "The secret things belong to the LORD our God, but the revealed things belong to us and to our children forever, to observe all the words of this teaching (this *tôrâ*)."

Although mysteries remain hidden, God makes the revealed things

---

8. Cf. Exod. 33:17; Num. 12:6-8; Deut. 34:1-10.

9. Samuel E. Balentine, *The Hidden God: The Hiding of the Face of God in the Old Testament* (Oxford: Oxford University Press, 1983).

accessible and near at hand to human knowing, a kind of knowing that leads to loyal commitment and active obedience.

> Surely, this commandment that I am commanding you today is not too hard for you, nor is it too far away. It is not in heaven, that you should say, "Who will go up to heaven for us, and get it for us so that we may hear it and observe it?" Neither is it beyond the sea, that you should say, "Who will cross to the other side of the sea for us, and get it for us so that we may hear it and observe it?" No, the word is very near to you; it is in your mouth and in your heart for you to observe (Deut. 30:11-14).

In the Deuteronomic vision that nearness and accessibility of God's partial but sufficient truth is accomplished through two means: a written scripture that contains the wisdom of the dead (the book of the teaching, or *tôrâ*, of Moses) and new words from the LORD that will be spoken through a new prophet like Moses. Moses promises Israel that, after his death, "the LORD your God will raise up for you a prophet like me from among your own people; you shall heed such a prophet" (Deut. 18:15). The truth of these new prophetic voices will be judged alongside the "book of the *tôrâ* of Moses" (Deut. 31:9-13). The interplay of a Mosaic written tradition and the possibility of new prophets suggests a fruitful balance and dialogue between the relative stability of a written tradition and the dynamic possibilities for new words from God.

Such renegotiations of older traditions are already embodied within the Pentateuch itself in the gradual merging and juxtaposition of varied traditions (for example, the earlier Yahwistic and later Priestly traditions) in Genesis-Numbers, and then the addition of the quite distinctive voice of the book of Deuteronomy, to form the full Pentateuch. Moreover, the final chapters of the book of Numbers (chapters 26–36) focus on the theme of a new generation of Israelites who are born in the wilderness and now prepare to enter the new promised land of Canaan. These chapters highlight the new generation's faithful reinterpretation and renegotiation of older traditions, laws, and narratives for its new time and circumstances. This new generation on the edge of the promised land functions as a paradigm for each succeeding generation of the future, honoring the past but also renegotiating its traditions in the face of new realities.[10]

In Deuteronomy, the written "book of the *tôrâ* of Moses" (a designation that tradition eventually extended to include not only Deuteronomy but the entire Pentateuch) recognizes itself as a secondary — and humanly mediated — tradition. The only primary, unmediated, and directly written words of God in the Pentateuch are the two stone tablets containing the Ten Commandments, which the text reports were the only words "written with the finger of God" (Deut. 9:10). These stone tablets engraved by God were placed prominently "in" the so-called ark of the covenant. The ark was a box, or shrine, that Israel carried through the wilderness and eventually placed in the Holy of Holies in the Jerusalem temple. Whereas the stone tablets were kept in the ark, Moses instructs the Levites that his book of the *tôrâ* should be placed beside the ark (Deut. 31:26). This placement — *alongside* the ark and not *in* it — was a sign of the derivative and secondary authority of Moses' book of the *tôrâ* relative to the Ten Commandments. At some point, the stone tablets of the Decalogue (written, according to the text and to tradition, by God's own finger) and the ark itself disappear off the stage of Israel's history, presumably during the Babylonian destruction of the Jerusalem temple or during some other destructive event. Thus we have only "the book of the *tôrâ*," a humanly mediated word of God, as an adequate though interpretive tradition by which each succeeding generation tests new words from God and seeks truth. Discerning truth in conversation with the biblical tradition is, like all human knowing, an interpretive process that is provisional and partial; but it is also adequate and sufficient to sustain the life and hope of a community of faith.

This partial and provisional character of the knowledge of God stems in large part from the divine habit of working in ways that run counter to human convention, expectation, and wisdom. Throughout the Pentateuch, God repeatedly defies human custom: time and again God chooses

10. Dennis T. Olson, "Negotiating Boundaries, The Old and New Generations and the Theology of Numbers," *Interpretation* 51 (1997): 229-40; and Dennis T. Olson, *Numbers: Interpretation Commentary* (Louisville: Westminster John Knox, 1996), pp. 157-93.

the younger sibling and not the expected eldest son for the chosen line; God also chooses to work through the barren woman, the slave woman, the foreign woman, the stranger, the alien, and the little ones (Num. 14) — those whose power is gone (Deut. 32). To know the truth about God requires a way of thinking and acting that runs counter to human expectations. What the apostle Paul said rings true of the God of the Pentateuch: "God chose what is low and despised in the world, things that are not, to reduce to nothing things that are, so that no one might boast in the presence of God" (1 Cor. 1:28-29).

4. The Pentateuch displays an openness to wisdom and truth outside itself.

Jethro the Midianite (that is, a non-Israelite) shares with Moses his wisdom about reorganizing the community as a means of redistributing judicial responsibility (Exod. 18). Moses asks Hobab, also a Midianite, to be Israel's guide on their march through the wilderness from Egypt to Canaan (Num. 10:29-32). What is remarkable is that this request for Hobab to act as a guide is juxtaposed to texts immediately before and after that highlight God's leading Israel through the wilderness by the pillar of cloud and the ark (Num. 9:17; 10:2, 33). The wisdom of a foreign human guide is portrayed in a complementary relationship with God's guidance and direction for the community. Elsewhere in the Pentateuch, a foreign prophet named Balaam speaks true oracles of blessing upon Israel (Num. 22–24), and an alien king and priest of Salem, Melchizedek, blesses Abraham by God Most High (Gen. 14:18-20). Jacob the Israelite looks into the face of his enemy and brother, Esau, the ancestral representative of the foreign nation of Edom, and says, "Truly seeing your face is like seeing the face of God" (Gen. 32:10).

Moreover, the Pentateuch's strong affirmation of God as creator of the world and its people, making covenant with them and all creation (Gen. 9:8-17), suggests that God may be at work generating truth and relationships among people of other nations in ways the Bible does not know or narrate. An example is Hagar, the Egyptian slave of Abraham and Sarah, and her son, Ishmael. This Egyptian slave woman is the only human in the Bible who names God ("You are ʾel roî [אל ראי] God who sees" — Gen. 16:13), and God promises to make of her and her son a great nation in a promise remarkably similar to the one initially made to Abraham and Sarah in Genesis 12:1-3 and then extended to their son, Isaac. Like Isaac, Ishmael would also become a great nation with innumerable descendants, and God would be with him (Gen. 16:10; 21:16-21). But the Bible does not narrate the rest of the Hagar and Ishmael story, though it leaves us to assume that God continued to be active among them — and presumably other peoples as well.[11] In Amos 9:7, for example, God informs Israel that God had performed exodus-like acts of deliverance and liberation for other nations besides Israel, nations such as the Ethiopians, the Philistines, and the Aramaeans.

It is interesting to note that, during the story of Israel's exodus itself, God is just as concerned that the Egyptians and Pharaoh know the truth about God's power and presence through the ten plagues as that the Israelites know (Exod. 7:7; 14:4; 14:18). Moreover, Moses' appeals to God's international reputation among the nations carry enormous weight with God. Moses asks God, for example, what the Egyptians and Canaanites will think if God destroys God's own people in the wilderness because of their rebelliousness at Mount Sinai (Exod. 32:12) and again at the edge of the land of Canaan (Num. 14:15-16). These appeals to the nations, along with other arguments by Moses, are sufficient to change God's mind about the judgments against Israel (Exod. 32:14; Num. 14:20). Thus does the Bible testify to God's interest in what truths the other nations know about God, and to God's often hidden activity among the other nations and cultures of the world.

Yet the proper use and integration of such wisdom and resources by communities of faith from outside the Bible and its traditions require discernment and testing. The Midianites did offer helpful wisdom (for example, Jethro and Hobab); but at other times they led Israel astray to worship other gods (Num. 25:1-18). The foreign prophet Balaam blessed Israel but then also participated in luring Israel into idolatry (Num. 31:16). The Egyp-

---

11. Ishmael reappears briefly in the Genesis narrative to join Isaac in burying their father, Abraham (Gen. 25:9). This is followed by a genealogical listing of Ishmael's descendants (Gen. 25:13-17). "Ishmaelites" appear in the Joseph narrative as caravan traders (Gen. 37:25-28) and are mentioned again in Judges 8:24.

tian gold the Israelite slaves took when they left Pharaoh and the land of Egypt (Exod. 3:21-22; 11:2-3; 12:35-36) came to use in building and adorning the tabernacle and the ark of the covenant, the seat of God's presence in the midst of Israel. (Early Christian interpreters used this biblical image of Israel's plundering of Egyptian gold for the tabernacle as justification for the church's plundering of Greek philosophy for use in Christian theology.) But this same Egyptian gold was also used to fashion the idolatrous golden calf at the base of Mount Sinai (Exod. 32:4). The resources and wisdom from outside the community have the potential to aid as well as corrupt the truth-seeking of God's people, and discernment is necessary in deciding how and when outside resources and guidance are usable.

5. The truth about God, self, and the world develops over long years of experience, struggle, suffering, and transformation within the context of God's chosen human community.
The nature of biblical truth is not understood as merely a set of propositions to which one can simply give or deny intellectual assent. I was a philosophy major in college, and one of my primary professors of philosophy was an ardent atheist. We became good friends and had many long and deep conversations about the existence of God and the nature of religious faith. He admitted that once, some years in the past, he had become convinced of the truth of Anselm's so-called ontological argument for the existence of God. Anselm argued that God is defined as "that than which nothing greater can be conceived." And since to exist in reality is greater than not to exist, Anselm argued, God must by definition exist in reality. My atheist professor was convinced by this argument for about a day or so. He believed God existed. But when he reviewed the argument the next day, he found what he perceived to be a flaw in the argument — so he changed his mind. He reported to me that, even when he believed in God's existence for those twenty-four hours, he felt no feeling of love or trust or fear toward the deity; he felt no inclination to pray to or worship or otherwise engage God. It was just a matter of a cold, rational decision either for or against the proposition "God exists." Needless to say, my philosophy professor had not captured the fully existential character of the Bible's understanding of truth.

For the Pentateuch, truth is primarily about moving into a deeper relationship and understanding of God over a long period of time — sometimes a very long time. Abraham asked the question aching in his heart after years of waiting for a child and a land that God had promised: "Oh LORD God, how am I to know?" (Gen. 15:8) How was Abraham to know who God truly was? How was he to know that God's seemingly impossible promises would come true? He was old, and his wife was barren. It took Abraham decades of mistakes and detours, glimpses and signs, repeated assurances and dialogues with God before he reached the point of truly believing and trusting in the truth of God's promises. God finally gave Abraham and Sarah their one child of the promise, Isaac. But then God tested Abraham's faith once more, even to the unimaginable point of commanding him to sacrifice his only beloved son in obedience to God (Gen. 12–22).

It took Jacob decades in exile from his home and family, struggling with his twin brother, Esau, his uncle Laban, and even wrestling with and being crippled by God, before he came to a more mature understanding of the truth of God's blessing. Jacob came to see that divine blessing could be received only as a gift; divine blessing was not something he could achieve by his own strength or cunning. As a result, Jacob, who long sought only to grab what he could for himself, was able, for the first time in his life, to give away a gift and a blessing to someone else, to his enemy and brother, Esau. "Please," Jacob says to his brother Esau, "accept my gift that is brought to you, because God has dealt graciously with me" (Gen. 33:11; see Gen. 25–33).

It took Joseph decades of experiences such as nearly being killed by his brothers, being sold into slavery, and being imprisoned unfairly, to change from a seventeen-year-old brat who flaunted his status as his father's favored son and to mature into a leader within the empire of Egypt and a family member who could forgive his brothers. Joseph conveyed to his brothers the hard-won truth he had finally come to know: "As for you, you meant evil against me, but God meant it for good, to bring it about that many people should be kept alive, as they are today" (Gen. 50:20; see Gen. 37–50).

It took Moses a lifetime of experience as an Egyptian prince, then a fugitive and a refugee, a humble shepherd of sheep, and finally an embattled leader of a band of freed but rebellious slaves traveling forty years in the wilderness to develop as God's great prophet. And yet even the great Moses, because of the people's sin and his own sin, had to join his own generation as they died in the wilderness. Moses was privileged only to see the promised land of Canaan; God did not permit him to enter it (Deut. 1:37; 3:23-29; 32:52; 34:1-12).

If it took Abraham and Jacob and Joseph and Moses a lifetime of struggle and transformation, it sometimes took the people of Israel generations. The repeated rebellions and conflicts of the old wilderness generation led, in the book of Numbers, to their death in the wilderness. The old generation was prohibited from ever seeing the promised land of Canaan. But their death made way for a new generation of God's people, a generation who learned from the past, renegotiated its traditions, and moved on into the promised land of Canaan (Num. 13–14; 26–36).[12]

Much more could be said about the understanding of truth in the Pentateuch and throughout the entire biblical witness. But I have set forth these five themes or insights:

1. the ancient seeds of our postmodern challenges;
2. truth as a relational trust as well as a product of more objective testing;
3. the partial but adequate character of the human knowing of God;
4. the Pentateuch's openness to wisdom outside itself about God and the world; and
5. truth as moving into a deeper understanding of God through a lifetime of experience, struggle, and transformation.

I put forward these insights in the hope that we will be reminded to look more closely at the richness, complexity, and nuance that the books of the Torah may contribute to our "big, deep conversations" about the Bible and

---

12. Dennis T. Olson, *The Death of the Old and the Birth of the New: The Framework of the Book of Numbers and the Pentateuch*, Brown University Judaica Series (Chico, CA: Society of Biblical Literature, 1985).

truth. Through such conversations we continue to struggle together to seek the truth as the people of God, asking Abraham's age-old question, "Oh LORD God, how am I to know?" In the meantime, we look toward an eschatological future and truth, for which we hope and trust but do not yet fully know. In the words of the apostle Paul, "Now we see in a mirror dimly, but then we will see face to face. Now I know only in part; then I will know fully, even as I have been fully known" (1 Cor. 13:12).[13]

---

13. This chapter is a slightly revised version of my inaugural address as professor of Old Testament at Princeton Theological Seminary; it was published as "'Oh LORD God, How Am I to Know?' The Pentateuch and Contemporary Understandings of Truth," *Princeton Seminary Bulletin* 23 (2002): 86-99. I wish to thank faculty colleagues and students who have offered comments and suggestions, some of which have been incorporated in this revision.

True Words

NICHOLAS WOLTERSTORFF

In the first part of this chapter I will argue that truth is *not* the main issue when we are dealing with Scripture; in the second part I will suggest that truth *is* the main issue.

I

Many of those who accept the Bible as canonical, and do not study it just for its scholarly interest or literary merit, are fixated on whether what it says is true. Consider Harold Lindsell's *Battle for the Bible,* a book that I take to offer a paradigmatic presentation of that way of thinking about the Bible characteristic of American fundamentalism. The battle for the Bible, in Lindsell's account, is all about the truth of what's said. Lindsell understands liberals to be of the view that only some of what the Bible says is true; Lindsell himself holds that everything it says is true. From the very beginnings of fundamentalism in the early twentieth century, biblical inerrancy has been a central plank in its credo; and what fundamentalism means when it says that the Bible is inerrant is that all that's said is true.

It is also characteristic of my fellow philosophers in the Society of Christian Philosophers to take the truth of what's said as the central issue to be raised when we reflect philosophically on the Bible's canonical status in the Christian community. That is part of what leads some of those outside the society to characterize its members as fundamentalists. Very few are in fact fundamentalists. They do, however, resemble fundamentalists in that the bulk of them — or at least the bulk of the vocal ones among them — regard the central issue concerning the Bible to be the truth of what's said.

Mainline and liberal Christians are different. For them the central category in reflecting on the role of the Bible in the Christian community is not the category of truth but the category of revelation: the Bible is revelation, or it effects revelation. But revelation, whatever else it may be, is perforce revelation of what is the case. What is not the case cannot be revealed: I cannot, for example, reveal that I am twenty-five years old, since I am not. What is the case is not the same as the truth of what's said; but the two are obviously closely connected. So whatever may be their differences on other matters, in this respect the difference between fundamentalists and conservatives, on the one hand, and liberals and mainliners, on the other, comes to very little.

One of the aims I had in mind in writing my book *Divine Discourse* was to break the grip of these categories — the truth of what's said and what is the case — when reflecting on the Bible and its role as canonical in the Christian community. "Oh, the depth of the riches both of the wisdom and knowledge of God!" exclaims Paul in Romans 11. "To him be glory forever." Is this true? Is it the case? The question misfires because exclamations are neither true nor false. "Blessed are those who hunger and thirst for justice," says Jesus in Matthew's report of his Sermon on the Mount. Is this true? Again, the question misfires: to bless someone is not to say something true or false.

To fixate on the question "Is what's said true or false?" when dealing with Scripture is to distort profoundly what is actually there. When an assertion is made, it is appropriate to ask whether what was said is true or false. There are a great many assertions in Scripture, and I am all for raising the question of truth about those. But we also find in Scripture an abundance of questions, commands, optatives, blessings — you name it. If we approach any of these with the question "Is what's said true?" we are trying to force square pegs into round holes. "Sell all that you have and give to the poor," said Jesus to the rich young ruler. The issue this saying presented to him — and presents to us — is not truth or falsehood but obedience or disobedience.

My own proposal in *Divine Discourse* was that, instead of thinking of the Bible in terms of revelation, we think of it in terms of speech; second, that instead of giving priority to speech as symbol-system, we give priority to speech as action, as discourse; third, that within discourse we distinguish between locutionary acts and illocutionary acts; and fourth, that we introduce the concept of double-agency discourse, thereby enabling us to understand how it might be that God speaks — that is, performs illocutionary acts — by way of the writing and speaking of the biblical writers.

Assertions are a type of illocutionary act, but only one among many. If it is God's speech that we are reading and interpreting on a given occasion, and if we determine that God is issuing a command by way of the passage in question, then it makes no sense to ask whether what's said is true. And we evade the point of the discourse if we ask what the issuance of this command reveals about God. The point is to obey. I am standing on a ladder, holding the board, ready to nail it in place, and I ask you to hand me the hammer. Instead of handing it to me, you ask yourself, "I wonder what his asking that question reveals about Wolterstorff?" Infuriating! Hand me the hammer!

In the course of my discussion in *Divine Discourse,* I made the point that, though the issue I was discussing in the book was how God could speak by way of the human words of Scripture, it was by no means my view that the only thing the Christian community should do with Scripture is ask what God says thereby. We take the Psalms on our lips to speak our own praise, lament, and dismay; so too we take on our own lips the doxological passages of the New Testament. We allow the metaphors of Scripture to shape the way we see reality. And so forth.

I trust that my point is clear: we distort and abuse what the biblical writers say, and distort and abuse what God says by way of what the biblical writers say, if we fixate on the question of whether what's said is true. Don't get me wrong: that question is usually important when relevant. But often it is not relevant. We have to get over our monomaniacal fixation on truth and on what's the case when dealing with the Bible.

II

Now for the second part of my essay. Every now and then one hears biblical scholars, theologians, and others — perhaps sensing intuitively that there is something wrong with our preoccupation with the truth of what's said or the what's-the-case of what is revealed — suggesting that we need a new concept of truth. Or suggesting, alternatively, that we ought to use the biblical concept of truth. In my experience there is nothing so effective in straightening and stiffening the back of an analytic philosopher as this sort of suggestion. If the suggestion made is the former, that we need a new concept of truth, the philosopher replies that such talk is all confused. You can make up whatever new concept you want and call it "truth"; but that does not give you a new concept of truth. It just gives you a new concept to which, since you made it up, you can attach any word you wish, old or new. I do not get a new concept of duck by making up the concept, say, of a small hairy animal with a bill and a tail and webbed feet and announcing that this is a new and improved concept of duck. And if the suggestion we make is the latter — that we should use the biblical concept of truth — the philosopher first asks why exactly it is that we should do that; and she then points to the very large number of passages in the Bible — and it is a very large number indeed — in which the word "true" appears for all the world to be used in the very same way that the philosopher uses it, namely, as expressing a property that propositions have when they bear the requisite relation to what is the case.

But perhaps my fellow philosophers are too quickly dismissive here. Not that either of the two points they make is incorrect. But maybe these points do not settle the issue; maybe there is more to be said. And just maybe, when that more is said, the possibility of a mediating position opens up before us. In the New Testament we rather often find a speaker saying that he is telling the truth and not lying (three examples: John 8:44-45; Rom. 9:1; 1 Tim. 2:7). Similarly, it is rather often said about some testimony that it is true (two examples: John 19:35; John 21:24). These are the passages that the philosopher latches onto: truth is ascribed to something asserted. (I have come to suspect that something more is being said, or at least suggested, in some of these passages than just that the content of what is asserted bears the relation that makes for truth to what is the case. But let that pass.)

Let us now look at a small sampling of the many passages in which something other than conformity to the facts is ascribed to an assertion by the predicate "true," or in which the predicate is ascribed to something other than assertions. Let us start with what is closest to that and move to what is farthest away. I will confine myself on this occasion to the writings ascribed to John; and from among these, my examples will be drawn almost exclusively from John's Gospel. Given the prominence of the word *alêtheia* and its grammatical variants in these writings, that is not a severe limitation.

In John 5:31, Jesus says, "If I bear witness to myself, my testimony is not true; there is another who bears witness to me, and I know that the testimony which he bears to me is true." Testimony is, of course, expressed with the illocutionary act of assertion, and it can accordingly be judged as true or false — in the sense of being in accord with, or out of accord with, what is the case. It is most unlikely, however, that that is what Jesus had in mind here in saying that testimony to himself would not be true if he spoke it. Why would his speaking it make a difference as to whether it was or was not in accord with what is the case? Add to this Jesus' remark in John 8:17: "In your law it is written that the testimony of two men is true." Here, too, it seems unlikely that he is using the philosopher's standard sense of "true" (cf. 8:13-14).

In the first letter of John we find the writer saying: "I am writing you a new commandment, which is true in him and in you . . ." (2:8). Here that of which truth is predicated is no longer an assertion. Though it is still predicated of something that is said, the something said is now a commandment rather than an assertion. In John 3:21, Jesus says that "he who does the truth comes to the light. . . ." Here it is no longer even one or another sort of illocutionary act that is said to be true but an action of some other kind. Moving on, we get phrases such as "true worshipers" (4:23), "true vine" (15:1), "true God" (17:3). In these expressions it is no longer even actions that are said to be true. Closely related, we find it said that God is true (3:33, 7:28, 8:26). And lastly, we get Jesus' well-known saying: "I am the way, the truth, and the life" (14:6; closely related to 17:17: "thy word is truth").

What are we to make of all this? Is the writer just speaking loosely over and over — so that we are to make nothing of it at all? Alternatively, is the writer perhaps using a number of distinct concepts, and it just so happens that all these distinct concepts are expressed with the same Greek word (*alêtheia*) and its grammatical variants (and with our word "truth" and its grammatical variants)? Or again, is the writer perhaps using a distinctly biblical (Hebraic, Semitic) concept, which coincides only in part with the concept attached to our word "truth"? If this last were the case, it would seem that our translators are to be charged with seriously misleading us in translating all the occurrences of the Greek *alêtheia* with the English "truth."

Let me approach my own suggestion, distinct from all the above, by calling attention to what is rarely if ever noted by philosophers, namely, that you and I also regularly predicate the word "true" of things other than assertions. We regularly say such things as these: "he's a true friend," "she's a true leader," "he's a true Dutchman," "she's a true scholar," "he's a true student," "that's true north," "this is true coffee," "that was a true wish," "here's a true copy," "that was a true aim," "the daylily is not a true lily," and "that tractor over there is not a true John Deere B anymore because it has been modified." We speak of "being true to the facts" and of "being true to life." We may say of a portrait, "It's just not true to her." And we confess that Jesus was "true God and true human being." In the face of all this, the suggestion that there is some peculiarly biblical — or Hebraic or Semitic — concept of truth has no plausibility whatsoever. Our English word "truth," along with its grammatical variants, maps the Greek word *alêtheia* and its grammatical variants, as they are used in the New Testament, about as closely as one could wish.

But is the force of the words "true" and "truth" constant amid all these different uses? That is surely the assumption that we should begin with, acknowledging that we may be forced to give it up. So on that assumption, let's see whether it is possible to state that force. Some will want to introduce Heidegger into the discussion at this point. Heidegger and his followers claim that he has achieved the purportedly remarkable feat of recovering the deeply buried root of our concept of truth. I think he has done nothing of the sort. At least in *Being and Time*, Heidegger is merely as fixated on the truth of assertions as is your average analytic philosopher. His argument is that, rather than understanding the truth of assertions in terms of correspondence between propositional content (Frege's *Gedanke*) and a fact, we get rid of the idea of propositional content and think, in ontologically reductionist fashion, of a true assertion as involving nothing more than an exercise of our linguistic practice whereby some fact is disclosed, unveiled, uncovered, or revealed. Disclosedness, he says, is "the ontological condition for the possibility that assertions can be either true or false."[1]

Another suggestion that is rather often made, one to which I was myself previously attracted, is that the root content of the biblical concept of "truth" is that of keeping faith with someone or something, of being faithful to someone or something. The truth of a proposition would then consist in its being faithful to the facts. The old English word "troth" has this sense of being faithful to someone or something: for me to pledge you my troth is to pledge you my fidelity. But this will not do either, and for this simple reason: "true" is often used in Scripture, and in ordinary speech, when the idea of keeping troth or being faithful is simply not in view. A true vine is not a faithful vine: what would a faithful vine be? And a true Dutchman is not a faithful Dutchman. Whatever constitutes a true Dutchman is both more than that and different from that.

A third suggestion to be considered is what Anselm proposes in the opening eleven sections of his *De Veritate* ("On Truth"). *De Veritate* is structured as a dialogue between a teacher and his student: the teacher and the student together take note of a wide range of applications of the predicate "true" — pretty much as wide as what I've pointed to above. And in each case they explore what "true" means in the application under consideration. The conclusion they reach is that in each case truth amounts to rectitude. And to say that something has rectitude is to say that, in the respect under consideration, it is as it ought to be. Here, from section 7, is a nice statement of that line of thought:

Teacher: But tell me if anything ought to be otherwise than it is in the highest truth.

1. Martin Heidegger, *Being and Time* (New York: Harper and Row, 1962), p. 269.

Student: No.

T: Therefore, if all things are what they are there, they are without doubt what they ought to be.

S: They are truly what they ought to be.

T: And whatever is what it ought to be, exists rightly.

S: It cannot be otherwise.

T: Therefore, whatever is, exists rightly.

S: Nothing is more obvious.

T: Therefore, if truth and rectitude are in the essence of things because they are that which they are in the highest truth, it is certain that the truth of things is rectitude.

S: Nothing is plainer than the consequence of the argument.

And here is another passage making the same point, this from section 10, when teacher and student are beginning to draw the discussion to a conclusion:

T: You will not deny that the highest truth is rectitude.

S: There is nothing else that I can say it is.

T: Consider . . . all the foregoing rectitudes are such because they are in things which are or do what they ought. . . .[2]

From the course of the discussion it is clear that, in arriving at and stating his general thesis, Anselm is employing the "ought" of proper formation and functioning rather than the "ought" of obligation; he thinks of obligation as a special case of proper functioning. After servicing one's car, the mechanic claims that it ought to run much more quietly now; this is the "ought" of proper functioning, not the "ought" of obligation. Two of Anselm's own examples of oughtness, or rectitude, are that sentences ought to be grammatically well-formed, and that sentences, when used assertively, ought to be true. Anselm's suggestion comes close to accounting for the examples I have put on the table, much closer than either of the

2. I am quoting from the translation by Ralph McInerny in Brian Davies and G. R. Evans, eds., *Anselm of Canterbury: The Major Works* (Oxford: Oxford University Press, 1998).

other two suggestions I have considered. But there are still a few examples that escape its net. When I say that the daylily is not a true lily, I do not mean that it is a malformed lily — that it is not what it ought to be. And when I say that a story is true to life, I do not mean that it is properly formed.

So let me now offer my own suggestion, which comes rather close to Anselm's. I suggest that the root notion of truth is that of something's measuring up — that is, measuring up in being or excellence. A true friend is one who measures up with respect to the quality of his friendship; true coffee is coffee that measures up with respect to its flavor or composition. When we speak of "a true so-and-so," we are implicitly drawing a contrast between this so-and-so that measures up and other so-and-so's that do not, or would not, measure up. What exactly that contrast is, will differ from case to case. A daylily is not a true lily because, though its flowers are definitely lily-like, it does not belong to the family *Lilium* and thus is not a lily at all. By contrast, a person who is not a true student is still a student — or then again, she may not be. One has to gather from the context what contrast it is that the speaker had in mind, and hence what sort of failure to measure up he meant to call attention to.

It is striking how often, in the New Testament writings ascribed to John, the contrast with what does not measure up is made explicit: there is a contest going on between the true and the not true — the true God versus all the false gods, and so forth. The exception to the point I made above about context determining meaning is that some phrases of the kind "a true so-and-so" have acquired a standard sense, so that, in the absence of contrary indications, the listener naturally takes the speaker to have in mind that way of measuring up that has become part of the sense of the phrase. This strikes me as being the case, for example, for the phrases "a true copy" and "a true [carpenter's] square."

Back to where we began, namely, with assertions. True assertions take their place along with true Dutchmen, true lilies, true coffee, and so forth, as things that measure up, in being or excellence, to whatever way is operative in the context, with this qualification: "true assertions," like "true copies" and "true squares," have long ago acquired a standard sense, with a particular way of measuring up built into that standard sense. That standard sense is this: a true assertion is one whose propositional content fits, or corresponds to, the facts. Or on the Heideggerian analysis: a true assertion is one that discloses the facts — one that is, as we say, true to the facts. In the absence of counter-indications, the listener assumes that the way of measuring up built into that standard sense is the way of measuring up that the speaker has in mind.

But a speaker need not use "true assertion" in the standard sense. I suggested that when Jesus said that, were he to testify to himself, it would not be a true testimony, he had something else in mind than the standard sense for "true testimony." He had in mind some other way in which a testimony given by himself concerning himself would not measure up. What that other way was, he did not say; we have to gather what it was from context. I once heard a sermon on the Massacre of the Innocents that began thus: the massacre of the innocents was a case of child abuse; in our society there is also child abuse; let us then talk about child abuse this morning. I submit that, though each assertion the preacher made was true in the standard sense, nonetheless the totality of what he said was profoundly false.

Truth is the fundamental issue to be raised concerning Scripture. Do the words of Scripture measure up? Are they true words? "Oh, the depth of the riches both of the wisdom and knowledge of God. . . . To him be glory forever." Is that exclamation a true exclamation? Does it measure up? "The Lord is my shepherd; I shall not want." Is that expression of confidence a true expression of confidence? Does it measure up?

Pursuing the Truth of Scripture: Reflections on *Wolterstorff's* Divine Discourse

BEN C. OLLENBURGER

In the few years since its publication, Nicholas Wolterstorff's *Divine Discourse* has received much critical acclaim, justified in my view, and has been put to constructive use in theological and hermeneutical proposals.[1] Wolterstorff was not the first to use speech-act theory in relating biblical interpretation and theology.[2] But his use of it, along with modes of analysis at home in contemporary philosophical theology, moves the discussion forward on several fronts. At the same time, Wolterstorff hopes to rehabilitate Scripture-reading practices that could be described as premodern. Those practices, as Wolterstorff describes them, and the arguments he advances on their behalf, will be the principal concern of this chapter. I will not attempt here to summarize all of the many and complex arguments in *Divine Discourse*. For example, I will not consider his arguments about and (for his purposes) against revelation and Karl Barth, his

1. As examples, see R. Lundin, C. Walhout, A. C. Thiselton, *The Promise of Hermeneutics* (Grand Rapids: Eerdmans, 1999); Joel B. Green and Max Turner, eds., *Between Two Horizons: Spanning New Testament Studies and Systematic Theology* (Grand Rapids: Eerdmans, 2000). Wolterstorff's *Divine Discourse* receives assessment in, among many other places, Timothy Ward, *Word and Supplement: Speech Acts, Biblical Texts and the Sufficiency of Scripture* (Oxford: Oxford University Press, 2002).

2. Cf. Ronald F. Thiemann, *Revelation and Theology: The Gospel as Narrated Promise* (Notre Dame, IN: University of Notre Dame Press, 1985).

arguments with and against Paul Ricoeur and Jacques Derrida, or his discussion of "entitlement," even though these form some of the most bracing chapters in the book. However, in what follows I attempt broadly to characterize several crucial components of his argument, as I understand them. Subsequently, I offer critical observations on some of these components. Finally, I proceed to some remarks more directly on the subject of Scripture and truth. *Divine Discourse* contributes to that discussion both directly and indirectly — or obliquely, as I hope to show.

The Methodological Argument of *Divine Discourse*

It is appropriate that Wolterstorff begins his book with an extended reference to Augustine, since *Divine Discourse* is a kind of late-twentieth-century version of *On Christian Doctrine*, with Augustine's "word, sign, and thing" giving way to "noematic content," "designative content," and "illocutionary stance," while retaining Augustine's cardinal interpretive criterion: love of God for God's own sake, and love of neighbor, or of anything else, for the sake of God. The point of Wolterstorff's early reference to Augustine is, of course, to introduce the notion of divine discourse — of God *speaking.* Hearing the words of a child — *tolle lege, tolle lege* ("take, read") — Augustine believed that he was being addressed by God, that is, he believed that God was *speaking* to him. But what is it to speak? Following J. L. Austin, Wolterstorff argues that to speak is to perform an illocutionary action. Not coincidentally, to speak — even when the speaker is God — is "to take up a normative stance" (p. 93)[3] and to "acquire the rights and duties of a speaker" (chap. 5). In speaking or discoursing, God performs illocutionary acts; significantly for our purposes, God performs such acts when discoursing through the medium of Scripture. Indeed, the many people who inscribed the words of Scripture were themselves performing illocutionary acts thereby. While Wolterstorff argues that some of these

---

3. All page numbers in the text of this essay refer to Nicholas Wolterstoff, *Divine Discourse: Philosophical Reflections on the Claim that God Speaks* (Cambridge: Cambridge University Press, 1995).

people — prophets and perhaps apostles — were deputized to speak for God, so that their discourse counts as God's discourse, Wolterstorff's principal concern is with human *appropriated* discourse and divine *appropriating* discourse. (He freely acknowledges, by the way, that one may have other, entirely legitimate, interpretive interests.) Scripture counts as divine discourse in case God appropriates its discourse, or in case God has, at some time in the past, appropriated it.

Apparently, God's appropriation of the Bible, specifically the Christian Bible, occurred in the past, since "the event which *counts* as God's appropriating this totality as the medium of God's own discourse is presumably that rather drawn out event consisting of the Church's settling on the totality as its canon" (p. 54). In other words, it is not that God *now* appropriates the Bible, or the human discourse within it, but rather that God *did* this appropriating over the first four centuries. And it follows that the divine discourse mediated by the appropriated human discourse is also past divine discourse; that is, Scripture as appropriated by God mediates what God was saying. Wolterstorff is largely consistent in using the past tense when referring to divine discourse by appropriation (see p. 216).

By contrast, when he refers to "*contemporary* divine discourse," to God's speaking to us now through the medium of Scripture, Wolterstorff invokes the notion of "presentational" discourse: God's presenting a text to someone, for example, to Antony. Antony overheard a lector reading from Matthew and, like Augustine after him, found himself immediately persuaded that he was being addressed by God. God spoke to Antony by means of presenting him with a text. Presenting someone with a text and discoursing that way is different from authoring a text. Of course, God did not author the Gospel of Matthew; according to tradition, Matthew did that. In so doing, Matthew engaged in an act, or in acts, of discourse.

At the same time, by means of appropriation, God is ultimately the author of Scripture. So we should want to find out what God was saying — that is, what God was saying as "a function . . . of those *human acts of discourse*" performed by however many people wrote the books of the Bible, or "authorized them in their present form to count as *their* discourse" (p. 186). Doing so naturally requires that we practice authorial-discourse interpretation. I say "naturally" because, if divine discourse is a function of human discourse, and thus of illocutionary actions, it follows that finding out what God said requires that we correctly interpret those illocutions — that is, discern their noematic and designative content, and also the illocutionary stance taken toward that content.[4] But taken by whom? Well, by the human beings — call them authors — whose acts of inscription generated their acts of discourse, that is, the biblical texts so considered.

This sort of argument leads Wolterstorff to a defense of authorial intention, which he rightly regards as heretical in certain circles. In this context he argues against Ricoeur and Derrida, among occasional others, including Hans Frei. For some of us, the mention of authorial intention conjures up a hermeneutical tradition whose aim or motto was "to understand an author better than he understood himself," a motto that appears in both Kant and Schleiermacher, but also in Ricoeur. Ricoeur's use of the motto is, oddly, congruent with Eric Hirsch's revision of his own argument for authorial intention *contra* Ricoeur. Ricoeur says that to understand an author better than he understood himself is "to display the power of disclosure implied in [the author's] discourse beyond the limited horizon of his own existential situation."[5] Hirsch includes among an author's intentions that of addressing future generations, so that a text's "originating moment in time" fixes "only the *principles* of further extrapolation." In other words, according to Hirsch, texts can bear meanings that were not at all part of their authors' consciousness.[6] It seems, then, that insistence on

---

4. If different speakers, speaking literally (in appropriate circumstances), assertively utter "Regina mortus est," "De koningin is dood," and "The queen is dead" (Wolterstorff's examples), the noematic content of their illocutionary actions is the same. If (still speaking literally and assertively, in appropriate circumstances) one speaker says, "The queen is dead," another "The regent is dead," and a third "The monarch is dead," the noematic content of the three illocutionary acts differs, but their *designative* content is the same (pp. 138-39).

5. In Hirsch, "The Model of the Text." I am quoting from Hans Frei, "The 'Literal Reading' of Biblical Narrative in the Christian Tradition," in *The Bible and the Narrative Tradition*, ed. Frank D. McConnell (New York: Oxford University Press, 1986), p. 52. Ricoeur expands on and modifies the point in *Interpretation Theory: Discourse and the Surplus of Meaning* (Fort Worth: TCU Press, 1976), pp. 75-79.

6. Hirsch, "Meaning and Significance Reinterpreted," *Critical Inquiry* 2 (1986): 627-30. I am quoting from Mark Brett, *Biblical Criticism in Crisis* (Cambridge: Cambridge University Press, 1994), p. 24.

textual autonomy and insistence on authorial intention can come to just about the same thing. In any event, Wolterstorff does not resurrect a hermeneutics that seeks to discover and then to be guided by the subjectivity of the author (p. 93) or what Dilthey called "schriftlich fixierte Lebensäusserungen."[7] Neither does he countenance a textual autonomy that can dispense with authors and their intentions.

But why not? That is to ask, with regard to reading the Bible, why bother with authors and their putative intentions, since neither seem to be of any great importance within the Bible itself? (I have in mind, for example, the use of Hosea 11:1 in Matthew 2:15: Matthew appropriates YHWH's reference to a past event involving Israel as a prophecy regarding Jesus. In other words, Matthew disregards Hosea's illocutionary posture and adopts an entirely different one toward the same locution, while giving Hosea's locution a new designative content.) The answer again lies in Wolterstorff's governing conception and proposal: (1) that God discourses, or discoursed; (2) that God's discourse is a *function* of human (i.e., biblical) discourse; and that (3) discoursing — "saying" (p. 199) — is an intentional action. Hence we make judgments about how, say, the anonymous authors of the Psalms operated their natural-language system for saying things, judgments based partly on "our beliefs as to which plan of action for saying something [t]he[y] probably implemented" (p. 199). We judge the illocutionary stance taken, based on verbal moods and genre. And, departing the text, we "enter the real world" to determine the designative content — what the discourser referred to. A lot depends, as Wolterstorff says, on our beliefs about the putative authors.

Some of this sounds like an apologia for what Wolterstorff, borrowing from Robert Alter, calls "excavative scholarship": biblical scholarship of a historical-critical sort. Indeed, Wolterstorff says it follows from his argument that "the work of scholars who open up to us a better grasp of what the human authors of Scripture were saying is of indispensable importance for the discernment of divine discourse" (p. 188). Of course,

---

7. See also Wolterstorff's remarks in "The Promise of Speech-Act Theory for Biblical Interpretation," in *After Pentecost: Language and Biblical Interpretation*, ed. Craig Bartholomew et al. (Grand Rapids: Zondervan, 2001), pp. 73-90.

Wolterstorff goes on to say that this scholarly contribution "finds its manifestation in the flow of new and better modern language translations," which he says has benefits for "ordinary readers." Whether or not this is the case — and whatever "manifestation" means here — Wolterstorff provides space for biblical scholarship, for "critics" (p. 202), in the discernment of human discourse. Besides producing good translations, perhaps biblical scholarship helps us to form sounder judgments about genre (see above) and about the biblical authors, or biblical discoursers: "Interpreters," he says, "cannot operate without beliefs about the discourser" (p. 196). And these judgments and beliefs will be indispensable to the discernment of divine discourse in the human discourse.

In this "second hermeneutic" ("interpreting for the mediated divine discourse") Wolterstorff again refers to authorial intention, and to the necessity of beliefs about the discourser. But in this case the author and discourser is God. And the medium of God's discourse is not a single text by itself, not even an entire book or a whole testament by itself, but the whole canon of Scripture. So an individual text will be read as part of the whole. But just as in the case of the first hermeneutic, interpreting the human discourse, the interpretation of divine discourse — judging what God said — has to proceed on the basis of our beliefs about the author, that is, our beliefs about God. In Wolterstorff's words:

> Interpretation of a biblical passage for the divine mediating discourse cannot proceed without the interpreter appealing to convictions she has as to what God would be likely to have intended by appropriating this passage within the whole text of the Bible. And such convictions . . . will depend crucially on what the interpreter believes about the nature and purposes of God (p. 221).

Critical Observations and Questions

A reader may be tempted to point out, in criticism of Wolterstorff, that Scripture is very much more than a medium of God's speech. For example, a congregation believes God to be present, and hence actively present, in and through its reading of Scripture (though not solely thereby) in such a way that God comforts those who mourn, heals the broken-hearted, creates faith, forgives sinners, and convicts the complacent. That is, God does not merely speak such things or promise them but actually accomplishes them.[8] I do not doubt that Wolterstorff would grant all of this, even as he grants to a variety of interpretive interests their own legitimacy. However, in *Divine Discourse* he focuses his interests on Scripture as the medium of God's authorial discourse, of God's speaking (or having spoken) by appropriation, and on the sort of interpretation that reads for this. That he does not consider other things cannot amount to a criticism. My critical observations and questions focus on what Wolterstorff actually aimed to do, so far as I understand this.

Among my puzzlements in reading *Divine Discourse* is its almost exclusive attention to sentences. For example:

I have assumed that for the determination of noematic content, the only considerations relevant are considerations about the meanings of sentences, considerations about tropic uses established in the linguistic culture, and considerations of probability and improbability as to what the discourser had and didn't have as his intention to say (p. 200).

My puzzlement increases when I try to extend this to the interpretation of texts of the kind that the Bible comprises.[9] I am conscious that those texts are made up of sentences. And I grant that each of these can be — perhaps must be — interpreted in something like the way Wolterstorff suggests. But then what? What about the rhetorical structure into which those sentences are fit, and the sometimes-suasive force of that rhetoric? I can, for example, perform on the book of Jonah at least some large part of the sentential analysis that Wolterstorff recommends — sentence by sentence — but still remain relatively clueless about the argument of the

---

8. I have elaborated this in "*Sola Scriptura*/No Other Foundation — and Other Authoritative Sources?" in *Without Spot or Wrinkle: Reflecting Theologically on the Nature of the Church*, ed. Karl Koop and Mary H. Schertz (Elkhart, IN: Institute for Mennonite Studies, 2000), pp. 65-92.

9. Ricoeur's remark that "a work of discourse is more than a linear sequence of sentences" seems on the mark here (*Interpretation Theory*, p. 76).

book.[10] And Jonah is a short book. There are wide disagreements about its argument, if it makes one, and disagreements about just how we should read it. As far as I can judge, the most Wolterstorff says on the matter is: "We . . . interpreters have to juggle tentative interpretations of the parts of the text until we arrive at the best interpretation of the total text — at that interpretation which has the highest probability of being the totality he [an author] intended to say with this total text . . ." (p. 205). But what lends itself to a ventured interpretation of Isaiah's "total text," based on frequently revised "tentative interpretations" of its parts, the quality of "highest probability" or any probability at all?[11]

I am unable to see in Wolterstorff's argument an obvious place for the various kinds of interpretation, rhetorical and otherwise, that biblical scholars engage in, and do so in many cases for theological purposes and with the church's uses of Scripture in view. It seems that the "dazzling contributions" (p. 202) that biblical critics have made stop short of all this, and the second hermeneutic takes over, discerning divine discourse. Of course, nothing prevents biblical scholars from proceeding to the second hermeneutic. But I am not complaining that Wolterstorff leaves the likes of me out of the interesting work; I'm wondering why the rhetoric of the texts (or their "narrative strategy," see Sternberg below) does not figure in the first hermeneutic, why textual interpretation is reduced to the interpretation of sentences.

10. Wolterstorff ascribes to the advocates of "textual-sense interpretation" (which he opposes: "[T]extual sense interpretation . . . is not a viable mode of interpretation" [p. 173]) the view that "the sense of a text is that totality of meanings which the sentences comprising the text have in that linguistic context which is the text" (p. 172). In other words, "the sense of a text is understood to be a function of the meanings of the sentences comprising the text; so that, for a given text, if one knows the sentences comprising the text and the meanings of those sentences, one knows everything necessary to determining the sense of that text" (p. 171). This very sort of thing Wolterstorff himself implies.

11. It seems to me that "probability" in this case, as in very many other (perhaps all) cases of biblical interpretation, should give way to "plausibility," for reasons similar to those cited by Bas C. van Fraassen on a different but closely related subject ("Three-sided Scholarship: Comments on the Paper of John R. Donahue, S.J.," in *Hermes and Athena: Biblical Exegesis and Philosophical Theology*, ed. Eleonore Stump and Thomas P. Flint [Notre Dame: University of Notre Dame Press, 1993], pp. 315-25, esp. pp. 320-21).

Second, if I am not mistaken, our judgments, or our beliefs, about the biblical discoursers or authors are formed primarily, though not exclusively, from the texts themselves, that is, from the discourse, or from the discursive or rhetorical achievement itself.[12] Authorial intention, then, is an inference we draw from the text — or a set of *ad hoc* hypotheses we make about the text — in the course of, and on behalf of, interpretation. But if we make *ad hoc* hypotheses about authorial intentions, or illocutionary stances, from the biblical text itself within our discourse-interpretive practice on it, then it seems to follow that we believe that the text suggests, constructs, or implies that sort of authorial intention, and thus that it justifies our beliefs about the kind of author who could have had those intentions we infer. In this regard, Meir Sternberg distinguishes between external and internal intentions: the former would include, among others, those Wolterstorff rules out (p. 93);[13] the latter, which Sternberg also calls "objectified" or "embodied" intention,[14] comes close to what Wolterstorff

12. Wolterstorff says as much: it is "by reading" that we make these judgments and form these beliefs. The full passage is quoted in the following note. We also employ considerations of or hypotheses about the "linguistic culture," as Wolterstorff says on p. 200 (quoted above).

13. On p. 93, Wolterstorff is discussing his "normative analysis of speaking," according to which "to speak is . . . to take up a normative stance in the public domain." He contrasts this with the notion that "to speak is . . . to express one's inner self." Connected with that mistaken notion is the "myth" that "to read a text for authorial discourse is to enter the dark world of the author's psyche. It's nothing of the sort. It is to read to discover what assertings, what promisings, what requestings, what commandings, are rightly to be ascribed to the author on the ground of her having set down the words that she did in the situation in which she set them down. Whatever be the dark demons and bright angels of the author's inner self that led her to take up this stance in public, it is that stance itself that we hope by reading to recover, not the dark demons and bright angels."

14. Sternberg says that "'embodied' or 'objectified' intention . . . fulfills a crucial role, for communication presupposes a speaker who resorts to certain linguistic and structural tools in order to produce certain effects on the addressee; the discourse accordingly supplies a network of clues to the speaker's intention." And intention "is a shorthand for the structure of meaning and effect supported by the conventions that the text appeals to or devises: for the sense that the language makes in terms of the communicative context as a whole" (*The Poetics of Biblical Narrative* [Bloomington, IN: Indiana University Press, 1985], pp. 8-9).

proposes. Because we have a text, we infer an author or a company of authors, even when, as in most biblical texts, no author is named. And by authorial intention we mean that set of *ad hoc* and revisable hypotheses we make about the illocutionary stance exhibited (or suggested) toward the noematic and designative contents of the text. Interpretation proceeds by, and as a form of, practical reasoning.[15]

Third, Wolterstorff's presumption ("presumably," p. 54) that the church's settling, after several centuries, on a canon of Scripture counts as the event of God's appropriating it as the medium of divine discourse remains underdeveloped. Many parts of the church no longer read the canon that God then appropriated: Carlstadt and then Luther, and the Protestant churches, generally "de-canonized" certain books and substituted for the Greek and Latin Old Testament a Hebrew Old Testament that was different in significant respects. Certain things that God said in the fourth century God apparently no longer said in the sixteenth century (and vice versa). Of more significance remains a matter to which I have referred above: that divine, appropriating discourse is what God said, at some time past, perhaps over the course of, or at the end of, the church's first four centuries, but also earlier and differently, in certain places, by virtue of, say, one of Paul's letters being read in Rome during his lifetime (pp. 55-56).[16] Christians seem — and indeed need — to be interested in what God is saying now, or in the case of preachers and prophets, what they should say for God, or for God's sake, and on behalf of God now. In all cases, Christians are interested in what we as Christians and as the church, before God, should be and do now — what kind of people we should be. Perhaps this depends on God's "confronting us with this [particular] passage of Scripture" (p. 238). May it be that presentation — ca-

---

15. Stephen E. Fowl, "Authorial Intention in the Interpretation of Scripture," in *Between Two Horizons*, pp. 71-87, esp. p. 76.

16. On p. 216, Wolterstorff expressly recognizes the issue, which leads him to frame the question appropriate to divine-discourse interpretation as: "What was God saying to us today by way of authoring this passage of Scripture?" Contrast Charles M. Wood: "Whatever else the church may make of these texts, it first attends to what God is saying through them, and takes this as their primary sense" (*The Formation of Christian Understanding: An Essay in Theological Hermeneutics* [Philadelphia: Westminster, 1981], p. 119).

nonical presentation, say — has priority over both deputization and appropriation? Perhaps it is through the manifold interpretation (p. 182) of the canonical witnesses to Jesus Christ (p. 291), and thus to the Triune God, that God speaks to, and against, the church. *Tolle, lege.*

Fourth, I harbor reservations about the way Wolterstorff constructs the relationship of the first and second hermeneutics. The distinction between them is rigorous and the relationship unilinear: one set of operations follows and depends on the other. The point, I gather, is to give the second hermeneutic, reading for divine discourse, firm and determinate ground in the first — reading for the human discourse. That point will be crucial if divine discourse is "a function of" the human discourse. We could not reliably judge what God said, then, apart from determinate judgments about what they said. Wolterstorff's argument here bears a formal resemblance to both the neologist J. P. Gabler's distinction between a first "true" and second "pure" biblical theology and Krister Stendahl's distinction between "what it meant and what it means." Each of them — though in different ways and to somewhat different ends — sought to distinguish a sphere of theologically disinterested and determinate interpretation (Wolterstorff might characterize it as "true" [cf. p. 181]) that could serve, by a separate operation, the waiting interests of theology.[17] It seems to me that Wolterstorff's argument is, in these places, susceptible of criticisms similar to those advanced against Gabler's and Stendahl's.[18]

---

17. Subsequently, Wolterstorff wrote that "[i]nterpreting Scripture for divine discourse is an inherently and unabashedly 'dogmatic' mode of interpretation" ("The Promise of Speech-Act Theory," p. 85). I have roughly concurred, in "Discoursing Old Testament Theology," *Biblical Interpretation* 11 (2003): 612-28.

18. J. P. Gabler, "An Oration on the Proper Distinction between Biblical and Dogmatic Theology and the Specific Objectives of Each," trans. Sandys-Wunsch and Eldredge, reprinted in *Old Testament Theology: Flowering and Future,* SBTS 1, ed. Ben C. Ollenburger (Winona Lake, IN: Eisenbrauns, 2004), pp. 498-506; Krister Stendahl, "Biblical Theology, Contemporary," *IDB* 1:418-32. I have discussed Gabler in several places, e.g., "Old Testament Theology: A Discourse on Method," in *Biblical Theology: Problems and Prospects,* ed. Steve Kraftchick et al. (Nashville: Abingdon, 1995), pp. 81-103; and Stendahl in "What Krister Stendahl 'Meant' — a Normative Critique of 'Descriptive Biblical Theology,'" *HBT* 8 (1986): 61-98. For criticism of the latter article, see Paul R. Noble, *The Canonical Approach: A Critical Reconstruction of the Hermeneutics of Brevard S. Childs* (Leiden: Brill, 1995), pp. 334-35.

To be sure, Wolterstorff proceeds to add considerable nuance to the two-staged functionalism he adopts in principle. That is, he imposes severe qualifications on his own claim that divine discourse is but "a function of" human (biblical) discourse. What we judge God to have said may, on occasion, differ dramatically from what we judge the textual medium of God's saying to have said. And these judgments will be informed decisively by our beliefs about God, and by other beliefs as well.[19] Wolterstorff describes a series of patterns to use in this regard (pp. 208-18), along with illustrations. Some of these resemble the rationalist (and neologist) strategies of two centuries ago, which interpreted for the main point, for the kernel of truth, discarding the rest as of "purely human significance," as husk (p. 210).[20]

It seems to me, any particular and concrete proposal regarding what God said, or may now be saying, by way of Scripture — any particular and concrete instance of theological interpretation or of proclamation, whether it assumes the form of preaching or of social witness, of liturgical celebration or private devotion — will, at least by inevitable implication, treat some part or aspect of Scripture, or some component of the passage(s) being interpreted, as of purely human significance and as husk. Given the diversity and comprehensive breadth of the church's, and of Christians', proper and (in some communities) required use of Scripture, judgments regarding kernel and husk, of divine discourse and human significance, will remain context-dependent, variable, revisable, and in every other respect contingent. They will remain so — precisely in light of our beliefs about God.

Here Thomas Aquinas may be suggestive, as when he affirms that the literal sense of Scripture is a matter of communal assent and opens onto a variety of "senses," consistent with God's being the author of Scripture.

---

19. For example, see his treatment of Psalm 93:1 (pp. 209-11). In this case, Wolterstorff does not rely only on beliefs about God. Instead, claiming that the verse betrays a geocentrism we know to be false, he rewrites it so that its designative content — what "the psalmist would surely have predicated of God" — conforms to what we otherwise know to be true of the world. So the affirmation about God ("everlasting") "is what we attribute to God." But that is not (all of) what the verse affirms, and what the verse principally affirms is affirmed about the world as God's creation. Geocentrism is not in view, here, by the way.

20. Gabler referred to this discarding as a stripping, an unclothing, an *Entkleidung*. See my "Old Testament Theology: A Discourse on Method."

Since Scripture's divine author "comprehends all things," the several senses potential within the literal or commensurate with it fall within the author's intention (*Summa Theologica* I.1.10, 13). Hans Frei seconded the notion of communal assent while refining the definition of literal sense, and Kathryn Tanner both interprets and expands constructively on Frei.[21] In any event, determining the normative or literal or otherwise religiously significant sense(s) of Scripture — or, to put it differently, the theological interpretation of Scripture — has always been a communal and thus also a political and moral practice, related to more or less explicit ends and purposes. The history of interpretation, hence (à la Ebeling) the history of the church, amply demonstrates that those ends and purposes can be corrupted, and with them the "moralities" that surround (and then corrupt) interpretive practices. (I will have more to say about this below.)

To his enduring credit, and in spite of the occasionally individualistic, sometimes heroic, tone of *Divine Discourse*, Wolterstorff fully recognizes that interpretation will be enhanced, and that beliefs may be reformed, through mutually self-critical engagement with diverse "others" (p. 238 and elsewhere). And consistent with his insistence that "God is in the details," he acknowledges that the textual details to which biblical "critics" draw relentless attention "resist imposed interpretations" (p. 202). These details, too, may compel us to recognize that our beliefs, including our beliefs about God, were in some instances mistaken (p. 238). In these and other ways, *Divine Discourse* bears on the subject of "Scripture and truth."

Scripture and Truth

According to Wolterstorff, the Bible may "say" things that are not true: it may assert falsehoods; that is, some of its human statements or propositions may be false. Perhaps many of them are false. But this does not mean that God, in appropriating (parts of) these sentences, has said something

---

21. Frei, "Literal Meaning"; Kathryn Tanner, "Theology and the Plain Sense," in *Scriptural Authority and Narrative Interpretation*, ed. Garrett Green (Philadelphia: Fortress, 1987), pp. 59-87. See Stephen E. Fowl, *Engaging Scripture: A Model for Theological Interpretation* (Oxford: Blackwell, 1998), pp. 38-39; "Authorial Intention," pp. 83-84.

false. Wolterstorff believes that God may well assert something that is false (or at least "not strictly speaking true" [p. 314, n. 7]).[22] However, God may have appropriated a false assertion in the Bible to assert what is true.[23] This relaxes somewhat our anxieties about the truth of Scripture. In the end, when he moves beyond the discussion of sentence meaning — namely, in considering the illocutionary stance of the Gospels — Wolterstorff arrives at a more supple understanding of the relationship between Scripture and truth. He arrives there by way of considering works of contemporary "not-exactly" or "not-only fiction," arguing that the Gospels are a kind of biographical portraiture in which there is "more truth of the kind we care about" than in a photograph or in the work "of a modern historian of the traditional sort" (pp. 258-59).[24]

But what kind of truth do we, or should we, care about? As many kinds as there may be, surely; but perhaps the phrase "kinds of truth" is infelicitous. Beyond the framework of his argument in *Divine Discourse*, Wolterstorff has in "True Words" (Chapter 2 of this volume) proposed that "the root notion of truth is that of something's measuring up — measuring up in being or excellence."[25] In some cases, Wolterstorff insists, the qualifier "true" has "long ago acquired a standard sense." This is so in the case of assertions: "A true assertion is one whose propositional content fits, corresponds to, the facts."[26] Otherwise, different ways of measuring up will be

---

22. Perhaps Wolterstorff will one day explain whether God's asserting what is "not strictly speaking true" would be to "abuse trust," to violate the "implicit compact" that speaking assumes and depends on (p. 89). On that topic, however, see 1 Kgs. 22 and Ezek. 20:24-26.

23. Origen, decidedly premodern, and Spinoza, harbinger and exemplar of the decidedly modern, had illustratively contrasting ways of regarding what is false — or does not qualify as true — in the Bible. Between them, Wolterstorff promotes a third way.

24. Francis Watson argues similarly in *Text and Truth: Redefining Biblical Theology* (Edinburgh: T&T Clark, 1997), pp. 60-63.

25. Wolterstorff, "True Words," an essay first delivered at the Christian Theology and the Bible Group session on "Scripture and Truth" (AAR/SBL Annual Meeting, Denver, CO, Nov. 17, 2001). The essay is Chapter 2 of this volume, and my quotations are from pp. 42-43.

26. I should note that Wolterstorff does not offer this as a theory of truth, much less defend it against a host of rivals or enter debate about the sense of "the facts." He is reporting a "standard sense," though, to be sure, in a way that displays his keen awareness of the

"operative" in different contexts; such measuring up will thus be assessed according to different criteria of being or excellence. In typical cases, something is said to be true by way of a contrast with something that, or someone who, does not measure up: a daylily is not a true lily, for example, because "it doesn't belong to the family Lilium and thus is not a lily at all." Similarly, a Pennsylvania Dutchman is not a true Dutchman because his proximate origins are in the German Palatinate and not in The Netherlands; he's not Dutch at all. Finally, or nearly so, Wolterstorff offers the example of a sermon — on the Massacre of the Innocents — in which "each assertion the preacher made was true, nonetheless the totality of what he said was profoundly false." Here I take Wolterstorff to mean that the propositional content of each of the relevant assertions fit, or corresponded to, the facts; yet the sermon, which included those individually true assertions, said something not true at all. The sermon, then, did not measure up. To put the point another way, the sermon was faithless. But faithless to what? Presumably, it was at least faithless to Scripture. Was it also faithless to God?

Finally, then, Wolterstorff asks: "Do the words of Scripture measure up? Are they true words?" The examples he provides with this question, asking also if they are true words, are not assertions; they comprise a discrete exclamation of praise (Rom. 11:33) and a discrete confession of faith and trust (Ps. 23:1). It would seem that, at least to a theologically significant degree, these words measure up — that is, that they are true — only if Scripture measures up, and not just with some of its "words" but in its totality. Is Scripture true? Does it measure up? Granted that some of its assertions are not true,[27] does Scripture indeed measure up? Is it faithful to God?

How would we go about answering that question? In one sense, *Divine Discourse* already presupposes an answer. If God appropriated the Bible as a medium of divine discourse, then Scripture must be, in the most impor-

---

debates and his stake in them — as, for example, in his reference to "the propositional content of assertions." Bruce Marshall takes a different (Tarski-Davidson) approach in *Trinity and Truth*, Cambridge Studies in Christian Doctrine (Cambridge, UK: Cambridge University Press, 2000). Lorenz B. Puntel provides an earlier survey across philosophy and theology, with his own proposal in "Der Wahrheitsbegriff in Philosophie und Theologie," *Zeitschrift für Theologie und Kirche*, Beiheft 9 (Tübingen: Mohr, 1995), 16-45.

27. See Wolterstorff, *Divine Discourse*, pp. 209-11.

tant respects, faithful to God — if only by God's decision that it be so. Traditionally (i.e., in some traditions), the way you go about answering questions of the "is such-and-such true of/faithful to God?" kind necessarily involves asking whether it is faithful to Scripture. For example, "Is the Belgic Confession faithful to God?" Since those who issued it did so "to prove that . . . adherents of the Reformed faith were . . . citizens who professed the true Christian doctrine according to the Holy Scriptures," I suppose they meant that it was faithful to God in the same way, and insofar as, it was faithful to Scripture.[28] That is, the confession presupposes Scripture's faithfulness in such a way that Christian doctrine constructed "according to" it would be truly Christian and thus faithful itself to God. Then where would the question "Is Scripture faithful to God?" arise? That is, does it measure up in just that way? Is Scripture true?

Intellectual developments over the centuries, perhaps especially the past four, have pressed searching questions about whether Scripture is indeed faithful to God. Certain of these developments have helped to reshape some of our convictions about the way in which Scripture measures up (i.e., is true). Perhaps it would be more helpful to speak of questions regarding how and when our uses of Scripture — and which uses of Scripture, in which circumstances — are true and faithful to God.[29] This will doubtless include reading Scripture in order to discover something, including what God was saying and would say. But it includes more. In this chapter I have typically referred to *Scripture,* rather than simply the Bible, because I have in mind the use of the Bible *as* Scripture, and thus in and by the church: by Christian communities in the service of their praise and penitence (p. 132), and by Christians to order their individual and common lives to the ends and purposes of God. Christian convictions about the truthfulness of Scripture (that Scripture measures up in excel-

---

28. The quotation is from the introduction to the Belgic Confession, published on-line at http://aztec.asu.edu/worship/celebration/creeds/belgic.html, accessed 1/25/00.

29. In some Protestant scholastic understandings, Scripture remains "efficacious even apart from its use *(etiam extra usum)*" (Carl E. Braaten, "Prolegomena to Christian Dogmatics," *Christian Dogmatics* [2 vols.], ed. Carl E. Braaten and Robert W. Jenson [Philadelphia: Fortress, 1984], 1:67). The notion may be salvaged by emending it to say that, even when it remains unused, Scripture remains potentially efficacious.

lence and is indeed faithful to God) are thus embedded in the church's variously doxological practices, especially within its liturgical practices. Liturgical practices, too, have and embody standards of excellence; they are patient of being assessed for their truth.[30] Scripture itself will figure indispensably in that assessment. However, "Scripture's fundamental authority is simply the fact that its *viva vox* is present in the church, and so present as to shape her life," says Robert Jenson, for whom it follows that the "primary doctrine of Scripture may be stated: *privilege* this book within the church's living discourse."[31] Within its liturgical practices, Scripture is the medium of God's active presence. Not the only medium, and not only of God's presence — but also that, so the church confesses.

If this is so, if our convictions about Scripture's truthfulness are embedded in Christian practices, then the question "Is the Bible faithful to God?" will be, in some large part, the question "Is the Christian community faithful to God?" Is its testimony true — and true to God?[32] This theological question cannot be pursued independent of the testimony itself, or independent of Scripture, because Scripture itself forms an integral part of the testimony. Apart from Scripture, the witnessing community cannot name the God on whose name it calls, to whom it testifies, and whom it praises — to whom it thereby professes truthfully to refer (ontologically).[33]

Wolterstorff offers a number of remarks about "performance interpretation," including that defending a sample of such interpretation, or

30. I have elaborated these points in "We Believe in God . . . Maker of Heaven and Earth," *HBT* 12 (1990): 64-96; and, drawing on Alasdair MacIntyre and David Kelsey, in "Theory and Practice in Theological Education," *The Aims and Purposes of Evangelical Theological Education*, ed. Paul Bassett (Grand Rapids: Eerdmans, forthcoming).

31. Jenson, *Systematic Theology*, 2 vols. (New York: Oxford University Press, 1997, 1999), 2:273. Elsewhere, Jenson suggests that, for derivative theological purposes, belief that the canon is "adequate" will suffice (*Systematic Theology*, 1:28). Cf. Ollenburger, "Sola Scriptura/No Other Foundation — and Other Authoritative Sources?" *Without Spot or Wrinkle*, pp. 65-92.

32. Bruce Marshall pursues this question from a different perspective in *Trinity and Truth*.

33. See Gerald Loughlin's discussion of Frei and Lindbeck, in *Telling God's Story: Bible, Church and Narrative Theology* (Cambridge, UK: Cambridge University Press, 1996), pp. 156-61; cf. James Fodor, *Christian Hermeneutics: Paul Ricoeur and the Refiguring of Theology* (Oxford: Clarendon Press, 1995), pp. 296-304.

"realization of a text" (p. 180), will amount to assessing "its value for this or that sort of person." Authorial-discourse interpretation, by contrast, will be assessed according to whether it is "correct" or "true" (p. 181). I am not yet persuaded on the point, for the reasons that follow.[34]

First, Wolterstorff has not yet shown how an authorial-discourse interpretation of some pericope or of some larger textual unit, perhaps one so large as a biblical book, may be assessed as true, except as it involves sentential analysis of noematic and designative content plus illocutionary stance, on the one hand, and large-scale, transtextual illocutionary-stance analyses (those he offers as characterizations of the Gospels), on the other. These analyses will be more or less plausible. As sentential analyses, they will often be uncontroversial, and hence correct, but they do not yet amount to a "realization" of the text (p. 178).

Second, performance interpretation, in the way Hans Frei exemplifies it (pp. 179-80), permits and encourages judgments regarding truth or correctness ("true" and "correct" are synonymous for Wolterstorff: p. 181) in the same measure as does authorial-discourse interpretation. Indeed, Frei would have had no principled difficulty incorporating authorial-discourse interpretation within the "tradition of the *sensus literalis*" (p. 179); he expressly permitted any "readings" that did not contradict the rules of 1) literally ascribing just to Jesus and predicating just of him Scripture's various descriptions; i.e., Jesus does not stand for or represent something or someone else, or nobody at all, and so forth; and 2) affirming the unity of the Christian Scripture's two testaments, so long as this affirmation respects the first rule.[35] Frei and Wolterstorff appeal to formally similar criteria — "value and disvalue," as Wolterstorff puts it (p. 181) — in making

---

34. See also Merold Westphal, "Review Essay: Theology as Talking About a God Who Talks," *Modern Theology* 13 (1997): 535; Shannon Craigo-Snell, "Command Performance: Rethinking Performance Interpretation in the Context of Divine Discourse," *Modern Theology* 16/4 (2000): 475-94.

35. Frei, "Literal Sense," pp. 37, 68-69, 42. As Frei expressed it in another place, "The predicates are what they are, singly and together, because they are his [Jesus'], and in the way they are his. He is not simply an embodiment, not even *the* embodiment, of one or all of the predicates that describe him" (*Types of Christian Theology*, ed. George Hunsinger and William C. Placher [New Haven: Yale University Press, 1992], p. 85).

their recommendations. And both appeal to the ages-old practice of Christian interpretation, which they seek to rehabilitate.[36] But neither invokes "value or disvalue" as an adequate or sufficient criterion of any particular interpretation. As Wolterstorff insists, "correct" serves appropriately as an approbation of performance (pp. 176, 181).

Third, I would like to extend the notion of performance interpretation, or that kind of realization of a text, beyond the limits Wolterstorff imposes on it. His discussion of the subject depends, in some part, on a lengthy quotation from Ricoeur, who employs the example of an orchestra conductor obeying the instructive notations of a score (p. 175). Ricoeur makes this analogous to a reader before a text: "The text is like a musical score and the reader like the orchestra conductor who obeys the instructions of the notation."[37] Wolterstorff substitutes his own analogy: "The counterparts of performers of scores are readers of texts . . . the counterpart of actually performing the score is reading through it and imagining things said with the words one reads" (p. 178). I propose to expand both Ricoeur's analogy and Wolterstorff's; or rather, I want to endorse Nicholas Lash's familiar proposal: "The fundamental form of the *Christian* interpretation of Scripture is the life, activity and organization of the believing community."[38] Performance interpretation in this sense — "performing the text," as Lash puts it — "enacts the conviction that these texts are most appropriately read as the story of Jesus, the story of everyone else, and the story of God."[39]

Wolterstorff makes the acute observation that "being guided in musical performance by a score is not a case of trying to find out something —

36. In *Divine Discourse,* Wolterstorff says that reading the Bible as a medium of God's speech was "the dominant practice in the Christian community for about 1500 years," and that it "is more viable than customarily supposed" (p. 131). In explaining his characterization of Frei as a performance interpreter, Wolterstorff suggests (if I read him correctly) that the matter turns on how Frei defends literal-sense interpretation. "The issue [for Frei] is whether the practice shows 'continued validity'" (p. 179, quoting Frei's "Literal Sense," p. 37).

37. Ricoeur, *Interpretation Theory,* pp. 75-76.

38. Lash, "Performing the Scriptures," in *Theology on the Way to Emmaus* (London: SCM, 1986), p. 42 (emphasis his).

39. Ibid.

though it presupposes having done that" (p. 175). The point holds for performance interpretation as well, on Lash's account of it. But this is so precisely because performance interpretation in this sense may be, and in fact demands to be, assessed as correct or true (or not).

> It follows that, for the practice of Christianity, the performance of the biblical text, to be true, it must be not only "true to life," but "true to his life;" and not only "true to his life," but "true to God." That it is so, and may be made so, is at once our responsibility, our hope and our prayer.[40]

The question "Is the Bible true?" understood as "Is the Bible faithful to God?" will be, in some large part, the question "Is the Christian community faithful to God?" Is its testimony true, and is it true to God? Along the lines Lash sets out, we should understand the testimony of the Christian community as embodied witness, and the community itself as an enacted commentary on Scripture.[41] Our questions about Scripture's truth invite and entail communal self-criticism — before God and thus also in the company of Scripture.[42]

Finally, then, I would like temporarily to invert the prevailing logic of "Scripture and truth," or "truth and the Bible," which assumes that the question involves the truth of the Bible. To do so, I will invoke the hermeneutics of suspicion, but in the form that Merold Westphal has given it. Concerning the "role of suspicion" he says: "It provides tools, for those willing to use them, for unmasking the false pursuit of truth."[43] Unlike

---

40. Ibid., p. 45.

41. I suggested this understanding in "Biblical and Systematic Theology: Constructing a Relation," in *So Wide a Sea: Essays on Biblical and Systematic Theology*, ed. Ben C. Ollenburger, Text-Reader Series 4 (Elkhart, IN: Institute for Mennonite Studies, 1991), pp. 111-45. John P. Burgess has recently adopted the same terms to somewhat different ends (*Why Scripture Matters* [Louisville: Westminster John Knox, 1998], pp. 120-40).

42. In addition to Fowl's *Engaging Scripture*, see Fowl and L. Gregory Jones, *Reading in Communion: Scripture and Ethics in Christian Life* (Grand Rapids: Eerdmans, 1991).

43. Merold Westphal, "Phenomenologies and Religious Truth," *Phenomenology and the Truth Proper to Religion*, ed. Daniel Guerrière (Albany: SUNY, 1990), p. 121.

skepticism about the truth or value of beliefs and practices, "suspicion" (as Westphal uses it) subjects to critical assessment (he says "challenges") the integrity of communities who so believe and practice. As one of the church's practices, theology has this "suspicious" responsibility: to expose the church and its practices to considerations of truthfulness, and to do so in the interpretation of Scripture. It will not consist *only* in the interpretation of Scripture, to be sure, but also and necessarily in that. And since, as Wolterstorff aptly points out, our beliefs about God (and also about ourselves and the world) bear heavily on our interpretation of Scripture, we must expose these beliefs to suspicion (p. 238), not only regarding their truth or justification but also regarding the social, political, and economic uses to which we put them.

"It is the praxicality of truth," Westphal says, "that makes it impossible to identify correct belief . . . with truth." And he offers this judgment as an interpretation of Scripture, specifically Jeremiah 22:13-16 and Romans 1:5; 16:25-26. These texts, he says, point to "the practicality of truth": that is, "to know is to do."[44]

> Moreover, the doing in question is not at all practical in the most familiar senses of the term. It is not practical in the technological sense of using intelligence to discover and employ the most efficient means of achieving my (our) ends. The doing is rather a self-transformative activity intended to bring me (us) into conformity with God's ends. It resembles Aristotle's *phronesis/praxis* more than it resembles his *techne/poiesis*, though the link to God's ends distinguishes biblical praxis from Aristotle's.[45]

Perhaps the activity will not be wholly "self-transformative," since none of our works are — all on their own. Even so, impractically and concretely conforming ourselves to God's ends, in "the obedience of faith"

44. Ibid., pp. 122, 107. In order to avoid "the instrumental and realistic" (i.e., self-interestedly practical) associations of the "practicality" he is talking about, Westphal introduces the term "praxicality."

45. Ibid., p. 107.

through the power of the Spirit, will remain more probative than otherwise attempting to confirm our convictions about Scripture's truth, which may receive substantial confirmation as a happy consequence. So we do well to exercise a certain suspicion. We should exercise it, for example, toward Augustine, who found his hermeneutical rule of love to be compatible with encouraging Rome's lethal suppression of dissenters, and toward Jean Gerson, who found his ecclesial "hermeneutics of tradition" compatible with, and even to require, the state's execution of Jan Hus.[46] But we do well to exercise this suspicion especially toward ourselves, as Wolterstorff insists (p. 238), in viewing our own "false pursuit of truth." For this we need the help of one another, and of others besides.

46. Mark S. Burrows, "Jean Gerson on the 'Traditioned Sense' of Scripture as an Argument for an Ecclesial Hermeneutic," *Biblical Hermeneutics in Historical Perspective*, ed. Mark S. Burrows and Paul Rorem (Grand Rapids: Eerdmans, 1991), p. 166. Fowl, in a discussion of Augustine's sermon against the Donatists, glosses over the point (*Engaging Scripture*, pp. 91-95). Burrows likewise does not mention Gerson's determination that Hus should be executed, even while Gerson remained in Paris, as its university's chancellor, and before Hus could utter a word in his own defense (see the account of Hus's trial in Matthew Spinka, *John Hus at the Council of Constance* [New York: Columbia University Press, 1965]).

The Rule of Love and the Testimony of the Spirit in Contemporary Biblical Hermeneutics

MARK I. WALLACE

I come to the topic of this chapter by way of my early memories of trying to make sense of the Bible as a fledgling Christian person. In my teen years I came to the realization that I needed to find a belief system that could give my life value and purpose. Identifying myself as a Christian, undergoing baptism, attending services at a local church, joining a Bible study group for young people — all of these activities gave birth to my sense of a loving relationship with a God who cared for me through the gift of the Spirit and the blessing of Scripture.

During this time I tried to read and live out the teachings of the Bible as faithfully as I could. I memorized many of Paul's letters, including the book of Ephesians, and was especially struck by his call to readers in Ephesians 6 to put on the whole armor of God as a protection against evil forces. I did not read this passage as a figurative trope for spiritual conflict but as a direct command to me to become an evangelical warrior for God. So in preparation for school one morning, I decked myself out in the chain mail of God's legionnaires according to Paul's vision: I "girded my loins with truth" by writing "truth" in large block letters across the wide leather belt I was then wearing in keeping with the fashion of the times. For the "breastplate of righteousness" I donned a tie-dyed T-shirt with the word "righteousness" emblazoned on the front and back in bold red letters. I put on tennis shoes with the word "peace" written all over them to ensure that my feet were "shod with the preparation of the gospel of peace." The baseball cap I wore, now transformed into the "helmet of salvation," was identified accordingly, and I painted the big Bible I was in the habit of carrying around with the phrase "sword of the Spirit" in fidelity to Paul's martial description of proper Christian dress.

When my mother saw me ready to go to school in this strange Pauline costume, she screamed that she would not allow me to embarrass myself in this way and insisted that I change into normal attire. Sadly, I consented to her demands, remembering that Paul also says in Ephesians 6 that children are to be obedient to their parents. I sensed intuitively that my mother's insistence on my changing clothes carried more weight than my own robust attempt to interpret Paul's teachings literally — in order to be a better Christian witness to others. This intuition stemmed largely from my mostly inchoate conviction that a Christian should do whatever he or she can to promote charity and compassion in any given situation. I sensed that while, on the one hand, I might make a real splash at my high school with my quasi-military getup, my mother, on the other hand, would surely suffer distress over her son's increasingly strange behavior. In other words, I learned that the Bible makes sense when we read conflicting passages in a sort of point-counterpoint fashion with reference to some overarching principle of interpretation. In my case at the time, that principle was Jesus' love ethic.

My aborted mission to dress in literal obedience to Paul's dictum has taught me that discerning the theological truth of the Bible is largely a constructive rather than a descriptive enterprise. A reader does not uncover the hidden or latent sense of the Bible buried deep within its pages but rather creates meaning through a sort of gestalt process of making sense of one passage in relation to others by appealing to a third general principle that relativizes all other readings. Biblical reading, then, is a largely intertextual affair. It consists of weighing the relative merits of this or that interpretation in relation to some higher principle that helps one make sense of the individual medley — or sometimes cacophony — of the passages in question. Biblical reading always operates by means of a canon within a canon. Every reader tacitly or openly operates with a "working canon" concerning what she thinks is the correct hermeneutical yardstick by which to measure the relative merits of this or that construal of a particular passage. In my exchange with my mother, I sensed that there was a hierarchy of meanings within the Bible that allows a reader to give privileged status to one reading over another in fidelity to that hierarchy. That morning I learned a valuable lesson in biblical exegesis that has stuck with me ever since: biblical truth is not as obvious and straightforward as it may appear at first glance because the truth of the Bible can only be won by thoughtfully juxtaposing one interpretation over and against another through reference to a body of first principles or guiding rules that the interpreter considers to be self-evident and just.

I

My notion of biblical exegesis as a kind of rule-governed give-and-take is an alternative to traditional biblical criticism, which seeks to establish the meaning of the biblical texts in relation to the relative factuality of the events and sayings recorded in these texts. Traditional biblical criticism is thus a more "scientific" and less "theological" form of inquiry than the kind of intertextual reading strategy I am suggesting here. As an exercise in establishing the historical reliability of the biblical texts or even the authenticity of Jesus' sayings, biblical critics weigh the textual evidence based on certain time-honored principles.

One of these principles is the criterion of dissimilarity: biblical stories and sayings are judged to be authentic if they can be proven to be significantly dissimilar from typical events and expressions characteristic of the time and the culture in which the Bible was written. Norman Perrin notes, for example, that Jesus' use of the appellation "father" in addressing God is uniquely his own usage and is not found among other literary forms of address to God in and around the time Jesus lived. It is reasonable to assume, therefore, that Jesus actually used this familial name to refer to God. Biblical critics use this principle of dissimilarity as one of the bases of their interpretive endeavors.[1]

---

1. Norman Perrin and Dennis C. Duling, *The New Testament: An Introduction* (New York: Harcourt Brace Jovanovich, 1982), pp. 397-429.

Another one of these principles is the criterion of multiple attestation: particular biblical themes and emphases are ruled authentic when they appear across different literary genres and traditions. Using this criterion, Perrin argues, for example, that because Jesus' distinctive views of the end of history appear and reappear in a variety of literary forms of expression, it is reasonable to assume that Jesus himself — and not some latter-day editor of the Gospel texts — is responsible for these eschatological views. In the light of the historicity of his end-time teachings, therefore, Jesus is to be read as an apocalyptic salvation-bringer: the result is that an understanding of his futuristic message should be central to the interpretive process.[2]

But as interesting as these historically testable hypotheses regarding biblical authenticity are for academics and others, such readings fall short of actually construing the religious truth of the biblical witness — that is, what the Bible means in its fullness and integrity as a compelling theological witness to life's fundamental questions. Biblical studies, then, should go beyond historical criticism toward an explicitly theological hermeneutics. Biblical studies should press beyond the historical-scientific approach and embrace a self-consciously normative reading of the scriptural texts based on the kind of to-and-fro hermeneutic I am suggesting here. In my mind, the best way to accomplish this task is by way of an appeal to the Spirit as the inner teacher who guides the reader into a relationship with the truth of God's love testified to in the biblical witness.

Nicholas Wolterstorff's *Divine Discourse* is an important conversation partner in my thinking about the role of Spirit-guided, theological criteria for biblical reading. The purpose of *Divine Discourse* is to explicate the claim that God speaks — and becomes present to the reader — through the biblical texts. While at first glance this claim might appear to be another way of discussing divine revelation, Wolterstorff argues that the topic of God's speech should be interrogated on its own terms and not assimilated without remainder to a doctrine of revelation. Wolterstorff's focus on divine speaking leads to two orienting conclusions: the most adequate model for understanding divine discourse stems from illocutionary

2. Ibid.

speech-act theory, and the application of time-honored hermeneutical rules to the Bible makes possible the mediation of divine discourse.[3]

I find Wolterstorff's use of speech-act theory to be an illuminating approach to the problem of how God speaks in the Bible. According to J. L. Austin and others, much of our discourse has performative force in that it not only says something (the locutionary act) but also often does something in the saying (the illocutionary act), or it generates a certain effect in the saying (the perlocutionary act). The advantage of using speech-act theory in the interpretation of Scripture is that it reveals the fundamental dynamic of biblical meaning: the biblical texts do not merely communicate propositional content but also, through the agency of the Spirit, they propel the reader into a living confrontation with the God referred to by these texts. Wolterstorff convincingly argues that, beyond the communication of ideas and beliefs, the Bible actually makes present the reality of the divine life in the very process of being read.[4]

To his credit, Wolterstorff does acknowledge that many Scripture texts do not appear to be faithful means of access to God's presence in the midst of the reading community; he uses the example of the imprecatory psalms as a case in point.[5] When David writes that God's people will be "happy" when they take the "little ones" of Israel's oppressors and "dash them against the rock," it is impossible to believe that this so-called prayer of thanksgiving is either an instance of God's speech or a candidate for making God present to the reader through God's communication with the biblical writers. The imprecatory psalms violate the most basic moral and religious sensibilities of the biblical witness. These psalms seem to counsel a religiously sanctioned infanticide, so how can they be an instance of God's Word? One of the ways around this odious problem is to interpret these psalms figuratively, that is, not as literal commands to hurt children but as expressions of the spiritual anguish the writer feels over Israel's destruction by its enemies.

---

3. Nicholas Wolterstorff, *Divine Discourse: Philosophical Reflections on the Claim That God Speaks* (Cambridge: Cambridge University Press, 1995), pp. 1-57, 202-22.

4. Wolterstorff, pp. 171-82.

5. Wolterstorff, pp. 202-22.

To do this, Wolterstorff retrieves Augustine's hermeneutical principle in the *Confessions* and *On Christian Doctrine:* that hermeneutics must aim toward construing the meaning of the biblical texts in a manner consistent with a life of charity and other respects.[6] "Whoever, then, thinks that he understands the Holy Scriptures, or any part of them, but puts such an interpretation on them that does not tend to build up this twofold love of God and our neighbor, does not yet understand them as he ought."[7] Using this rule, Augustine goes on to say that any text that is *prima facie* incompatible with engendering love of and a right understanding of God and neighbor must be figuratively or metaphorically reinterpreted so that it cannot be read as promoting actions that are otherwise blasphemous or immoral. Augustine continues: "Whatever there is in the word of God that cannot, when taken literally, be referred either to purity of life or soundness of doctrine, you may set down as figurative. Purity of life has reference to the love of God and one's neighbor; soundness of doctrine to the knowledge of God and one's neighbor."[8]

In the case of the imprecatory psalms, then, since these passages violate the Augustinian rule of love, they do not make sense as genuine instances of God's speaking, according to Wolterstorff. Such texts, however, can be legitimately appropriated by the reading community as divine speech-acts when we reread them as vivid (if sadly misguided) expressions of pent-up fury against those who make war against God's people. Since killing children, for whatever reason, is always wrong, these texts are only redeemable as metaphor clusters that express the understandable anger of the biblical writer against his tormentors, not as endorsements of behavior that undermines the hermeneutical rule of love of God and neighbor.

I find Wolterstorff's felicitous use of Augustine's love hermeneutic to be especially relevant to the task of discerning scriptural truth in biblical studies. My thesis, then, is that biblical truth is the ethical performance of what the Spirit's interior testimony is prompting the reader to do in the light of her encounter with the scriptural texts. Attuning oneself to the

---

6. Ibid.
7. Augustine, *On Christian Doctrine*, I, 36, 40.
8. Augustine, *On Christian Doctrine*, III, 10, 14.

Spirit's promptings enables the "practice," "performance," or the "making" of the truth through "enacting" one's desire for the other's welfare. In addition to having a certain kinship with Wolterstorff's approach, this formulation of biblical truth bears deep affinities with Patrick Keifert's rhetorical model of truth in biblical reading.[9] For Keifert, the Bible is true insofar as it makes possible a rich and vital understanding of God through genuine Christian praxis — praxis that entails healthy congregational and family life in relation to caring for vulnerable others or the strangers in the midst of the community. In this model, discerning the Spirit's inner persuasions is coterminous with compassionate engagement with the other, even though this moral engagement does not have the security, as Keifert puts it, of an intellectual theory or foundation on which to base the rationality of such an engagement. There are no extracommunal warrants outside the process of Spirit-discernment — what the Reformed tradition valorizes as the *testimonium Spiritus Sancti internum* — that can apodictically ground the gesture of compassion toward the other.

In the Reformed heritage, John Calvin and Karl Barth both highlight the role of the Spirit's interior witness as crucial to the process of biblical understanding. They refer to the Spirit as the "inner teacher" *(interior magister)* who makes possible a deep and vital understanding of the Word of God through the words of the biblical witness. Both thinkers use the key pedagogical trope for the Spirit in Paul's writings, where the Spirit is figured as the divine tutor who educates the subject to the end that he will enjoy a productive relationship with the gospel. The Spirit is a necessary condition for the receipt of revelation, just as a good teacher makes real and accessible a body of knowledge to his students. Without the Spirit, the living power of the biblical message to renew and transform the reader is not possible. The testimony of the biblical texts to heal and refresh the reader is not realizable in the life of the individual unless the Spirit makes it happen. Calvin writes of "the saying of Paul's that the Ephesians had been 'sealed with the Holy Spirit of promise' [Eph. 1:13]. Paul shows the Spirit to be the inner teacher by whose effort the promise of salvation penetrates into our minds, a promise that would otherwise only strike the air

9. Keifert's argument is found in Chapter 8 of this volume.

or beat upon our ears."[10] Similarly, Barth writes about the "subjective reality of revelation" as the Spirit's role of making possible the reader's capacity for hearing and responding to God's offer of God's self through the biblical witness: without the Spirit, readers and listeners are tone-deaf to the divine offer. The Spirit makes possible one's ability to be a recipient of, and to act upon, the truth.[11] The objective reality of revelation, therefore, is God's self as God is made manifest through the Word within the words of the biblical witness; the subjective reality of revelation is the Spirit who prompts and leads human subjects into a transformed relationship with this living truth through their encounters with Scripture.

But what are the moral dimensions of this truth discernible through the Spirit's inner persuasions in the life of the reader? What is the Spirit urging readers to embrace as they struggle to grasp the meaning of the biblical witness? In short, generosity and compassion toward others is the moral ideal the Spirit urges on readers who seek to understand the biblical texts through the inner testimony of the Spirit. As God is love, so are we to love others. Love, then, is the overarching, hierarchical principle that mediates the competing readings generated by an intertextual reading strategy.

Along with Calvin's and Barth's emphasis on the Spirit, I put forward Wolterstorff's and Augustine's thought as reliable guides for crafting a biblical hermeneutic ruled by charity: the fulfillment and end of scriptural interpretation is the love of God and neighbor; any interpretation that does not accord with this principle is invalid no matter how "correct" or "accurate" the interpretation might seem to be, based on historical assumptions. For Augustine, God is an overflowing and plentiful "fountain of truth" who infuses the Bible with a plenitude of meanings — all of which have their origin in the common benevolent headwaters of the divine life itself. Thus a particular passage may contain an almost endless plurality of meanings, none of which can be definitively adopted based on "what the author meant" or "what really happened." For Augustine, appeals to authorial intent or historical verification can only partly unveil

---

10. John Calvin, *Institutes of the Christian Religion*, III, i, 4.

11. Karl Barth, *Church Dogmatics*, I/2, ed. T. F. Torrance and G. F. Bromiley (Edinburgh: T&T Clark, 1956-75), I/2, pp. 203-79.

the truth of the biblical witness, because biblical truth is primarily born by the edifying capacity of these texts to awaken the reader's desire to imitate divine love by loving God above all else and loving one's neighbor as oneself.[12] The Spirit summons the reader to live a life of ethical integrity and fidelity to the command to love God and serve one's neighbor. Augustine goes on to say that there may be an irresolvable ambiguity about what an author actually meant in a particular passage or whether an event actually occurred in the way narrated by the author. But these problems are of little consequence for Augustine; what matters in the end is whether the interpretation in question offends the rule of charity. If it does, such an interpretation cannot possibly be true regardless of its grounding in authorial meaning or historical events.

II

My case is that biblical truth consists in performing the Spirit's promptings to love God and neighbor. But if this is correct, then what is the status of the Bible's historical claims? If, as traditional biblical criticism maintains, no interpretation is adequate unless it is grounded in scientific evidence, what is the precise relationship between the Bible's historical claims, on the one hand, and its religious message, on the other? Some practitioners of contemporary Christian theology and biblical scholarship have anxiety about proposals of criteria for scriptural truth claims that do not fully embrace the factual, historical claims of the events recounted in the Bible. Various attempts have been made by such practitioners to secure the reliability of the biblical witness on the foundation of a common sense realist or historicist conception of truth in which the claims of the Bible — whether those claims be moral, historical, scientific, or eschatological — are judged to be "objectively the case" or "how things really are." In this historical-realist model, truth is a property of statements that accurately correspond to external states of affairs independent of the mind of the human knower. Stephen Davis makes this point well

12. Augustine, *Confessions*, XII, 32-43.

when he writes that the Gospels, for example, provide straightforward "factual assertions" about Jesus' life and ministry. Davis says that, unlike the genre of "imaginative history," there is "almost nothing in the Gospels as individual texts [that] make us want to think of them in this way. . . . Indeed, I think it is about as clear as anything can be that the evangelists believed, and wanted us to believe, that this is how things actually happened."[13]

I agree with Davis that the Gospel stories purport to tell us what happened in the life and ministry of Jesus. But because the point of these stories is not to chronicle (in the sense of modern-day historiography) every occurrence and utterance in Jesus' life, but rather to tell a historically embedded story for the purpose of the salvation of the world, I disagree with the claim by some realist theologians (though I do not think that Davis is among them) that to believe in the truth of the Gospel stories entails belief in every putative chronological and factual detail in these stories. The point of the Gospel narratives is to tell an ancient salvific narrative, not satisfy the standards of evidence for modern scientific history. This does not mean that the history-like character of the Gospel accounts is irrelevant to their meaning, as if — in the manner of Rudolf Bultmann — one could peel away the historically conditioned husk of the biblical message in order to uncover the timeless philosophical kernels of truth wrapped tightly within this husk. On the contrary, it is essential that the Gospels be read as history and not as timeless myth. But this affirmation forces us to ask a fundamental question: Precisely what kind of history do the Gospel narratives set forth?

On this question, Karl Barth's distinction between different kinds of biblical history is instructive. Barth makes a bipartite distinction between the "'historical' as historically demonstrable" *("historisch" als geschichtlich feststellbar)* and "narrativized history" *(erzählte Geschichte).*[14] "Historical" history stands for a record of events scientifically reconstructed through critical historiography: it is a chronicle of the past that emphasizes the historicity of particular events apart from the significance (cultural, religious,

---

13. Davis's argument can be found in Chapter 5 of this volume.
14. Barth, *Church Dogmatics,* I/1, pp. 324-30.

and so forth) attached to these events. Narrativized history, on the other hand, records history not in terms of an impartial chronicle but in terms of a culturally rich story where past events are remembered as charged with significance and meaning. Thus in the Gospel accounts, according to Barth, we have a narrativized history of events written with a particular objective in mind: to retell the Jesus event — God's self-disclosure and self-concealment in time and space — in order to persuade the reader to become a follower of this Gospel story. The thrust of these stories, then, is evangelical and rhetorical, not historiographical and scientific. The all-important claim of the narrative history of the Gospels is that divine revelation (what Wolterstorff calls "divine speech") has taken place in this particular place and time, not that the record of this occurrence is historiographically accurate in all of its details. As Barth says, "Thus, even if according to standards of modern historiography [narrativized history] does in certain instances, having no interest in this regard, commit 'errors' in what it says about the time and place, the important thing is not the more or less 'correct' content but the very fact of these statements."[15]

It is for this reason that Barth makes his now-famous claim that not all history is historical ("*Nicht all Geschichte ist historisch*").[16] He argues that the events set down in Scripture are faith-based testimonies to actual history-like occurrences, even if such events could not then nor can now be historically verified in a positivist sense. That these events are perceived and understood through the eyes of faith does not make them any less real or any less a part of history (*Geschichte*) even if, as Barth says, such events occurred at a time before the establishment of the canons for scientific, observable history (*Historie*). Glossing Barth, I am struck that what makes the Bible *true* is its paradigmatic capacity to serve as a trustworthy guide (in the sense of the Old English word *troth* or the Hebrew notion of *emeth*) for faith and practice even if it may not be, and probably is not, factually *accurate* in all of its particulars and details. Indeed, it may even be that our insistence on the historicity of all aspects of Scripture's narratives reveals, ironically, our residual fidelities to the pseudo-security of Enlightenment

---

15. Barth, *Church Dogmatics*, I/1, p. 326.
16. Barth, *Church Dogmatics*, III/1, p. 80.

standards of rationality rather than a Spirit-grounded biblical faith that should remain radically open to challenging the received knowledge and wisdom of the wider secular culture. Why should the rules of positivist historiography set the terms for a theological appropriation of the truth of the biblical witness?

Therefore, I do not think that historicism and realism are the necessary bulwarks for supporting religiously vibrant and historically rich interpretations of biblical truth for our time. On the contrary, I find the clarion calls in theology for realism — or antirealism, for that matter — to be beside the point. I believe that theories such as realism (truth as correspondent to mind-independent reality) or antirealism (truth as a matter of choice in regard to incommensurate conceptual schemas) are inadequate to an understanding of the biblical summons to the reader to love God above all else and exercise charity toward one's neighbor. Against the false juxtaposition of truth in realist-versus-constructivist terms, a performative model of biblical truth maintains that a theological judgment is valid whenever it enables compassionate engagement with the world in a manner that is enriching and transformative for the self and the other.

This model puts the emphasis on truth as the basis of action, as Augustine (and Wittgenstein, for that matter) puts it, not as a fit between mind and world (realism) or as the result of intracommunal agreement (antirealism). Of course, what does and does not count as "compassionate engagement toward the other person" is a difficult problem for the performative approach, and how exactly this approach differs from its close counterpart, the antirealist position, also needs to be sorted out. These questions notwithstanding, my proposal is driven by a conviction that in theology, at least, a belief is true just insofar as it fosters a life of love of God and benevolent regard toward one's neighbor. My hope in this approach is that the purpose of a biblically enriched theology will again be regarded (as it was for Augustine) as the art of scripting one's life in fidelity (in the sense of truth as *troth*) to the Spirit's promptings to love God and serve one's neighbor. Biblical truth, therefore, begins with the willingness to travel to meet the other in his need and destitution by following the path plotted by the Spirit in the heart of each person.

III

Let me now offer a practical example of how the love ideal works in an actual reading of the biblical texts. As a case study of my model for interpretation, I will look at two of the most pressing social justice and polity dilemmas that now confront many mainstream Protestant churches: the related questions of ordaining to ministry gay and lesbian persons, on the one hand, and blessing the unions of couples in same-sex relationships, on the other. In order to tackle these polity issues, however, it is important to first address the root question that underlies these difficult issues: What is the biblical understanding of homosexuality?

To begin, I should note that the Bible is generally negative toward homosexuality. Leviticus says that it is an abomination for a "man to lie with a man as with a woman," and Paul writes in Romans about "degrading passions," where women and men abandon "natural" relations with another and are instead consumed with passion for those of their own sex. Initially, therefore, it appears that the Bible is hostile to same-sex relations and that a sound theological ethic of sexuality for our time should ground its suggestions in Scripture's antihomosexual prescriptions. But if one reads the Bible intertextually rather than in isolated chunks, one notices quickly that the Bible's sexual ethics often do not make sense without the introduction of some overarching principle to sort out Scripture's conflicted moral teachings. For instance, the Bible condemns homosexuality, but it also condemns other practices with a severity that we now consider inhumane if not barbaric. What sense does this make? Consider that, in addition to its decrees on homosexuality, Leviticus also strictly prohibits sexual intercourse during a woman's menstrual period: violators of this prohibition are to be cut off from the community, that is, they are to be expelled by stoning, burning, or strangling. Deuteronomy condemns adultery, specifically a man who has sex with another man's wife; and here the punishment is death by stoning for both the man and the woman. Likewise, Jesus in the Gospels reserves one of his most strident and consistent denunciations for those who get a divorce: "What therefore God has joined together let no one pull apart" (Matt. 19:6). While Deuteronomy permits divorce in some cases, Jesus strictly forbids it, saying that if a person initiates a divorce, he or she commits adultery.

Many contemporary Christian groups today — on both the right and the left of the political divide — regard themselves as biblically centered in their promulgation of a consistent moral ethic. But while many of these groups have no problem with fellow congregants who have sex during a woman's period, get a divorce, or perhaps commit adultery at some point in their lives, they remain deeply conflicted about, if not outright opposed to, gays, lesbians, and transgendered persons. The inconsistency here is notable. Do we invade people's private lives and severely punish them for having sex during menstruation? Do we stone couples who have relations outside of marriage, as prescribed by biblical law? Do we, in keeping with Jesus' diatribe, stigmatize divorced people as sinners who have violated God's fundamental command against tearing apart what God has joined together?

In response to these questions, let's take the question of our attitude toward divorce today. Not only do we not label divorcees with a scarlet letter as sinners (which Jesus' clear condemnation of divorce might call for), but sometimes we recommend divorce as a healthy alternative to toxic relationships where one or both members of the relationship are not able to realize their God-given potential to live full and satisfying lives. In many cases we no longer regard divorce as sinful (again, Jesus' statements to the contrary notwithstanding) but as a potentially liberating life-passage event that can bring healing and renewal to both parties involved. Indeed, many churches now have blessing rituals for divorced couples and their families to help the aggrieved parties break their vows and leave their lifelong relationships on a mutually amicable note. And, in general, I think this shift in our thinking makes good sense. Virtually all churches extend full communion to divorced persons; divorced people and their families are candidates for baptism, marriage, and remarriage, and they are regarded as fit for positions of leadership (including ordination in my own denomination, the Presbyterian Church U.S.A.). Jesus was vigorously opposed to divorce yet said nothing about homosexuality. But while we may marry persons who have been divorced with the church's blessing and may accept them as potential leaders in local congregations, some people question — on religious grounds — the legitimacy of same-sex unions and ordination for gays and lesbians. Why this inconsistency?

The problem, in my opinion, is that we pick and choose from the Bible what best suits our presumptive sense of right and wrong, and then we read back into the Bible what we have already assumed to be there in the first place. Instead of exegeting out of the biblical texts their full-bodied and often conflicting teachings on human sexuality, we eisegete (or read *into* the biblical texts) what we expect to find there. Instead of honestly coming to terms with the teeming complexity that makes up the biblical witness, we import into Scripture our own anxieties and prejudices and then legitimate them by offering up proof-texts as their warrants. When we truly do read the Bible in its full complexity, without bracketing out what is offensive to our modern sensibilities, what we see are some very liberating — and potentially very dangerous — ancient customs and prohibitions that may or may not be relevant to our contemporary struggles to understand the nature of healthy human relationships. I am not suggesting that we dismiss the Bible and its sexual mores as irrelevant to our current questions; rather, I am suggesting that we read the Bible as an expansive, rambling, and ceaselessly oscillating intertext in which contrasting passages can only be understood in relation to some all-informing principle that helps to make sense of the sometimes dissonant and contradictory messages the biblical texts communicate to readers.

I have proposed the Spirit-inspired ideal of love and hospitality toward others as the hermeneutical lodestar that should guide our interpretive encounters with the wide-ranging expanse of the biblical universe. Like a tonal piano piece that requires a theme to inform the many combinations and permutations the melody and baseline undergo throughout the piece, so the Bible — if it is to be appreciated harmonically as a work of transformative art and not as a cacophony of noise and clamor — requires some organizing theme by which the reader can make sense of and appreciate the beauty of its music. Thus the call to love God and to love one another is the organizing theme of the biblical witness. When applied to the question of homosexuality, such an approach yields the conclusion that love and acceptance of our neighbor is the right way to make sense of the

Bible's diffuse and sometimes dated understandings of sexual relationships. Walter Wink puts this point well:

> [The Bible] exhibits a variety of sexual mores, some of which changed over the thousand-year span of biblical history. Mores are unreflective customs accepted by a given community. Many of the practices that the Bible prohibits, we allow, and many that it allows, we prohibit. The Bible knows only a love ethic, which is constantly being brought to bear on whatever sexual mores are dominant in any given country, or culture, or period.[17]

The Bible's love ethic is the coherent center of Scripture's witness. Thus the gesture of compassion toward the other person, whatever his or her sexual orientation, is the right foundation on which to ground all decisions concerning the church's faith and practice, including those decisions related to ordination for homosexual Christians, on the one hand, and blessing unions for same-sex couples, on the other.

Without the guidance of this love ethic, the Bible threatens to pull apart in a centrifugal explosion of hopelessly backward and contradictory messages. The love ethic is the centripetal force that brings together this potential Babel of many voices into a harmonious working relationship; it is the gravitational pull that reorients the polyphony of the Bible so that passages at odds with our deepest moral sensibilities, or in direct conflict with one another, can be reread as potentially complementary motifs in an ever-expanding symphony of meaning. Under the tutelage of the Spirit, the love ethic provides the center around which the wide variety of culturally bound and sometimes dated scriptural teachings can whirl and spin like so many planets around the sun.

17. Wink, "Homosexuality and the Bible," in *Homosexuality and Christian Faith*, ed. Walter Wink (Minneapolis: Fortress, 1999), p. 44.

IV

It is important to note that giving precedence to the rule of charity is critical for biblical interpretation not only because it helps us to understand Scripture's teachings about sexuality but also because it allows for the redemption, so to speak, of biblical stories that seem beyond the pale of God's will. But this redemption is hard won if it is won at all. Pulsing toward the inner witness of the Spirit, it becomes clear that significant sections of the Bible cannot easily be subsumed under the principle of God's love as the foundation for solicitude toward others. As we saw in the case of the imprecatory psalms, important biblical accounts do not at first glance seem to square with the Augustinian rule of biblical reading that God is love and all interpretation must be compatible with this maxim. The problem with the rule of charity is that, in the cracks and along the fault lines of the regnant biblical accounts of God's loving activity, another picture of God emerges for the reader aware of the troubling polyphony within the Bible. Like the God addressed by the angry writer of the imprecatory psalms, another face of God appears on the margins of the text: a taunting, capricious, and sometimes malign divinity who destroys a family because of a lie (Ananias and Sapphira in Acts), hands over the body of an innocent man to Satan for testing (Job), and unleashes the ultimate violence of sacrificial infanticide (the slaughter of the Egyptian first-born in Exodus). These stories of extravagant divine violence and vengeance call into question straightforward applications of the love principle to all aspects of the biblical witness.

Accounts of divine terror in Exodus, Job, Acts, and elsewhere take us to the borders of a hermeneutic of charity to the place where God's benevolent, covenantal identity is mocked by the caprice and malice that seem to lie close to the heart of God's self. Of course, we can ignore those borders by following instead the supreme Christological plot line to its predetermined *telos* in the final triumph of God over all things that are evil and anti-God. But such a road short-circuits the ambiguity and confusion that lie underneath and alongside the biblical narratives of love and grace, and it runs the risk of depriving the victims of radical suffering the complete literary space necessary for them to act out their anger toward and struggles with God.

The problem with the temptation to make a facile application of the love principle to Scripture is that it will delimit too quickly the possible traversals available to the reader who enters the Bible's literary universe. The risk is that this approach will ward off the chaos that resides in the recesses of the Bible's stories because it is embarrassed by their heterodox possibilities of meaning. The danger, in other words, is that a reading emphasizing compassion will take premature refuge in the comfortable literary space of the Jesus story that Christians have been taught to trust and rely on without coming to terms with the incursions of apparent divine malevolence in the Bible that stand outside the historic hermeneutical rule that states: "God never speaks nor acts contradictorily nor falsely nor in a manner incompatible with consistent charity toward the other."

Many readers who have struggled to live in fidelity to the Jesus story find that something is missing in a reading that immediately looks for the rule of charity in a passage. What is missing is the power of deep and strong readings of the biblical texts to refigure our entire experience as selves in the valleys of the shadow of death, the power of a vertiginous and sometimes healing freedom to read these texts in all of their plenitude and pathos and heterogeneity. Deep readings take the risk of going beyond conventional cultural mores and assumptions, and they refuse to cauterize the reader's pain by means of a truncated hermeneutic that issues in discipleship to a God whose identity is only on the surface of — and not underneath — the narratives. Charity implies that the mainline stories of God's gracious agency tell the whole story; but those who testify to the misery of others, or who themselves endure the pain of recalcitrant evil, know that the numbing enigma of massive, undeserved suffering remains inscrutable and unanswerable within the historic Augustinian hermeneutic of love of God and neighbor. Something is missing.

A more balanced — and I believe more biblical — handling of the issue of the Bible's own complicity in undeserved violence would be to read the biblical texts against themselves. In this model, the love principle is still regnant but in a fashion that is more sensitive to conflict and opposition than Augustine allows for. At times the Bible should be read against its own deep grain: to read the Bible against itself is to use the love ideal to elucidate the hermeneutical warfare at work within the biblical intertext itself. Through the power of the Spirit, readers must track how the Bible cuts back on itself — to find out how divine love and love for others is possible even in those Scripture passages that betray that love in violent portraits of God's relationships with humans. The point is to read the Bible against the Bible in the light of its own announced theme of antiviolence, even if that theme is frequently garbled by the texts undermining the very theme that they gave rise to in the first place. Such a criterion for a compassionate, antiviolent "working canon" provides a more honest acknowledgement of the mixed discourse at work in the Bible's conflicted avoidance of, and occasional capitulation to, the destructive language and mores it often condemns.

V

The Bible as a whole is an irreducible mixture of dated cultural material, sometimes violent stories, and incredibly rich and transformative suggestions for human well-being. Through the inner testimony of the Spirit, the use of a love hermeneutic helps the reader discern where the coherent truth lies in the Bible and what is peripheral to that central truth. I have said that the use of such a hermeneutic is not an uncovering of the Bible's hidden sense but rather a construal of its more liberating possibilities. Biblical meaning is not given in the words of the texts themselves but instead is produced on the basis of the reader's active engagement with the texts' projection of new possibilities for existence. Meaning is generated in the give-and-take interaction between text and interpreter; it is not a timeless property of the text that awaits discovery by the passive reader. In this sense, the burden of discerning the truth of the Bible can only be handled — as Luther always insisted, and rightly so in my judgment — by readers who self-consciously take a particular interpretive stance toward the Bible in the light of their own "working canon" or "hermeneutical template."

Understanding the Bible comes through pitting one passage against another vis-à-vis the overarching truths held dear by the interpreter. Biblical understanding consists of a ceaseless interplay of competing readings played out in relation to foundational assumptions that the interpreter considers to be bedrock to any right understanding of religion. That God is love and that we are enjoined to imitate God's love in compassion toward our neighbor is the bedrock assumption I believe liberates the Bible toward its own best possibilities, even as this assumption sets free the critique of the Bible when it becomes captive to the more debilitating mores of its own particular time and place. The biblical witness does not offer a coherent sexual ethic, nor is it an unyielding testimony to God's consistent graciousness. But at many critical points the Bible does shine forth with the radiance of God's compassion, and we can look to these flickers of light as illuminations of new ways of being in the world toward which the Spirit calls each of us.

What Do We Mean When We Say, "The Bible Is True"?

STEPHEN T. DAVIS

I

Suppose we wanted to capture part of our attitude toward the Bible with the statement "the Bible is true." What might we mean by this statement?

Let me begin with what I take to be three desiderata for a theory of "the Bible is true," that is, three things that such a theory must accomplish. First, such a theory must take note of our special human status as verbivores.[1] Every living organism has certain needs that must be met in order for it to survive and thrive: food, shelter, a method of reproduction, and so forth. But human beings are special among all the creatures in that we have an additional need, a need for words, particularly words from God. Thus Moses, speaking for God in Deuteronomy 8:3, says to the children of Israel: "One does not live by bread alone, but by every word that comes from the mouth of the Lord."[2] Second, such a theory must explain

1. I did not invent this term; so far as I know it was coined by Robert C. Roberts, "Parameters of a Christian Psychology," in Robert C. Roberts, ed., *Limning the Psyche: Explorations in Christian Psychology* (Grand Rapids: Eerdmans, 1998).

2. Notice also *Phaedo* 85d, where Plato has Simmias say: "It is our duty to do one of two things, either to ascertain the facts, whether by seeking instruction or by personal discovery, or, if this is impossible, to select the best and most dependable theory which human intelligence can supply, and use it as a raft to ride the seas of life — that is, assuming that we

why Christians read the Bible, as opposed to any other book. Why do we Christians hold the Bible to be unique among such classics as *The Iliad* or *The Koran* or *The Critique of Pure Reason?* Third, such a theory must explain why Christians take the Bible to be normative or authoritative. Why is the Bible a text and guide that it is not only appropriate but mandatory for Christians to allow themselves to be formed as persons by it?

To tip my hand, I believe it will turn out that a strong factor in satisfying all three desiderata is the notion that, in some important sense, God speaks to us in the Bible.

II

Now let's return to the statement "the Bible is true." What might this statement mean? This presents some difficulties for a philosopher: though we are well aware that there are other uses of the word "true," philosophers normally think that the only kinds of things that can be true (or false) in the paradigmatic or realist sense of "true" are things such as assertions, claims, statements, or propositions. This sense of "true" means "having the truth-value true," that is, being in accord with what is the case. Thus Aquinas's justly famous claim that "truth is the agreement between the idea and the thing."[3]

Accordingly, rocks, trees, numbers, galaxies, quarks, and books (such as the Bible) do not have truth-values and accordingly are neither true nor false. Of course, if a given statement can be said to be true, then surely a set of statements can be true, presumably if all the statements in the set are true. Thus we might say that someone's testimony about a certain event is true if all the statements made by the witness are true. Like-

---

cannot make our journey with greater confidence and security by the surer means of a divine revelation." *The Collected Dialogues of Plato*, ed. Edith Hamilton and Huntington Cairns (New York: Pantheon Books, 1963), p. 68.

3. Thomas Aquinas, *Quaestiones Disputatae de Veritat*, 1:3 (available in an English translation as *Truth . . . translated from the definitive Leonine text* [Chicago: Regnery, 1952-1953]). See also William P. Alston's magisterial defense of realism on truth in his *A Realist Conception of Truth* (Ithaca, NY: Cornell University Press, 1996).

wise, then, perhaps even a book could be true if all the statements in it were true.

But this does not seem to be a helpful route to follow in trying to decide what we might mean by "the Bible is true." For one thing, to say that the Bible is true in the sense that all the statements in it are true does not seem nearly to capture what orthodox Christians want to say about the Bible. To illustrate this point, we might imagine the following scenario. I decide to write a book that contains nothing but true statements — just as a lark. It contains sentences whose truth I know from experience, such as "grass is green" and "San Francisco is north of Los Angeles"; it also contains mathematical or logical truths, such as "7 + 5 = 12" and "all triangles have three sides." It also contains true statements about the past, such as "Lincoln was shot at Ford's Theater" and "the Pirates won the World Series in 1960." Imagine that this book is three hundred pages long and consists of nothing but one true statement after another. Notice that we could call such a book "true"; we might even call it "inerrant." But it would be a banal, pointless, virtually incoherent, and religiously useless book — in other words, quite unlike the Bible.

More importantly, the Bible consists of far more than assertions. (I emphasize this point because those who hold conservative views of the Bible are sometimes caricatured as holding that the Bible consists only of a set of propositions.) Everybody knows that the Bible contains all sorts of genres and linguistic elements — law codes, poetry, parables, songs, commands, questions, expressions of praise, exhortations, and many others — that seem incapable of being, in the paradigmatic sense, true (or false). I do not mean any of this to deny the importance of the fact that there are true statements in the Bible. There are obviously many narrative sections in the Bible, that is, where historical assertions are made; there are also many theological and moral assertions. Perhaps it is important for most, or even all, of these assertions to be true. It does seem difficult to grasp how a book replete with false claims could be considered authoritative. But what surely seems clear is that those Christians who want to express their attitude toward the Bible by the statement "the Bible is true" must mean a great deal more than simply, "Its assertions are all true."

Of course, the word "true" can be used in ways other than "having the truth-value of true." We sometimes use expressions such as "true to one-self," "true blue," "true north," "true feelings," "a true copy," and "to come true," and such expressions seem not to have much to do with "having the truth-value of true." "True" can also mean attributes such as loyalty, sincerity, trustworthiness, fidelity, giving helpful guidance, or proving accurate. And some of these usages are surely relevant to what we might mean by saying, "the Bible is true."

Still, I want to see whether we can make progress by sticking to something like the paradigmatic sense of "true." Let me ask this question: What psychological attitude do we have toward assertions that we regard as true, statements such as

San Francisco is north of Los Angeles,
$7 + 5 = 12$,
my wife loves me,
and (if we are theists) God exists?

And what psychological attitude do we have toward assertions that we regard as false? Part of the answer, I suppose, is that, in regarding statements that we take to be true, we commit ourselves to believe them (together with all propositions entailed by them), we accept their propositional content, we "trust" them, we "lay ourselves open" to them. That is, we allow our rational structures and behavior to be influenced by them; and we do not do any of that with statements we regard as false.

Let me suggest that we mean something like this when we say that the Bible is true: we mean that our attitude toward the Bible is such that we believe what it says, we trust it, we lay ourselves open to it. We allow our rational structures and beliefs to be influenced by it. Such an attitude will include but not by any means be limited to accepting the truth (in the paradigmatic sense) of the assertions that we find in it. (What they are, obviously, will have to be interpreted.)[4] It also means taking questions in the

---

4. Indeed, I should point out that in this chapter I am abstracting away from all hermeneutical questions in a quite arbitrary way. I know well that judgments about the truth of an utterance — whatever notion of "true" is envisaged — are parasitical on judg-

Bible ("Should we sin the more that grace may abound?") as legitimate and probing questions addressed to us. It also means taking biblical exhortations ("Give thanks to the Lord, for he is good") as exhortations addressed to us that we must heed. It also means taking poetic sections from the Bible ("We are his people, and the sheep of his pasture") as powerfully affective expressions of the way reality is.

If we take the Bible to be true, we trust it to guide our lives. We allow our lives to be influenced by it; we intend to listen where it speaks; we consider it normative; we look to it for comfort, encouragement, challenge, warning, guidance, and instruction. In short, we submit to the Bible, and we place ourselves under its theological authority.

III

Notice that some of the things I believe to be true, I believe more firmly than other things I believe to be true. For example, I believe the statement "the dean of the faculty respects me." After all, he and I have been friends and colleagues for years, and I think I know him and his opinions quite well. But I believe the statement "my wife loves me" much more firmly than I believe the statement "the dean of the faculty respects me." Now, I believe both statements, in fact; but I believe the one with a great deal more certainty than I believe the other. It will be much more difficult to convince me that my wife does not love me than to convince me that the dean does not respect me. Much more powerful defeaters will be needed.

Clearly, those who hold the Bible to be true in the sense we are using here — they trust it, listen to it, look to it, submit to it, consider it normative — believe the Bible to be true with a great deal of firmness or certainty. Their belief in it is not tentative; their submission to it is not halting. The Bible is allowed to guide their lives, influence their behavior, and form them as persons.

---

ments about the meaning of that utterance. Although I do make a few hermeneutical comments in Section VI of the paper, for the most part I am simply assuming that we know what various biblical utterances mean.

In one sense, this submission is quite voluntary. It's not as though somebody coerces Christians to submit to the Bible, as in the way most people obey rather quickly when a policeman says, "Put your hands behind your back!" But I do not want to give the impression that those people who in some strong sense submit their lives to the Bible do so randomly or capriciously; it is not like flipping a coin or choosing one flavor of ice cream over another. It's not like one person saying to another, "My holy book speaks to me, but somehow yours leaves me cold." Those who place themselves under the authority of the Bible do so precisely because they hold the Bible to be true. That is, they hold that the Bible is objectively authoritative. It is, as we might say, worth submitting to.

If I submit myself to the Bible, it has authority over me in one sense only because I take it as authoritative. (Note that it is possible for people to reject a given law — say, the law forbidding exceeding the speed limit — to regard it as having no authority over them.) But in another sense I take the Bible to be authoritative over my life precisely because I regard it as objectively authoritative. (Similarly, even those who choose to ignore the law forbidding speeding are under its authority and can be ticketed and fined.) The Bible is objectively authoritative, then, in that people *ought* to accept its authority, whether they do so or not.

In philosophy we say that every assertion or proposition has certain truth conditions, that is, the conditions that must be satisfied in order for the proposition to be true. The truth condition of "San Francisco is north of Los Angeles" is simply San Francisco's being located north of Los Angeles. Perhaps the linguistic utterances from the Bible that are not assertions (e.g., "Honor your father and your mother," "Pray without ceasing," "Praise God in the sanctuary") also have, in an extended sense, truth conditions. Reality must be in a certain way and not other ways in order for those biblical statements to be objectively authoritative. It must be the case that it is morally obligatory to honor one's mother and father; it must be the case that God commands us to pray without ceasing; it must be the case that God deserves our praise and that the sanctuary is an appropriate place to express that praise.

IV

There is nothing in the theory of "the Bible as true" that I am espousing that requires a defender of it to reject the theory known as biblical inerrancy. This is the theory that every properly interpreted assertion in the Bible — whether about theology, history, science, logic, sociology, geography, mathematics, or whatever — is true. Still, it is also perfectly possible to hold the theory without embracing inerrancy. To some people, that indeed might amount to one of its strong points. Early in my career I wrote a brief critique of biblical inerrancy in favor of what I called biblical infallibility.[5] Although I still embrace its overall approach, I now regard some of the arguments used in that book as unconvincing, and I am now familiar with more nuanced ways of understanding the concept of "biblical inerrancy" than were available in 1977. Still, my basic problem with the doctrine of inerrancy — and the reason that I do not defend it — is that commitment to it seems to drive interpreters of the Bible at various points toward forced, awkward, and even ridiculous interpretations of the Bible in order to make problematic assertions in the Bible come out true.

It is clear that a great many people do not regard the Bible as true in the sense just explained. (1) Some of them are atheists, religious skeptics, or enemies of Christianity who explicitly disbelieve what the Bible says, or at least much of it; and they certainly reject the crucial parts. (2) Others suspend judgment, in effect, on what the Bible says until there exists a scholarly consensus. This seems to be the attitude of many scholars of Scripture today; they consider the Bible to be no different in principle from any other ancient text — Plato's *Republic*, for example, or the Gospel of Peter. They believe what the Bible says only if historical-critical research substantiates it; that is, it is a wholly human book, like any other book. (3) Many other people these days have no idea what the Bible says and don't seem to care to know. Anybody who has taught undergraduates in secular colleges or universities in recent years is familiar with such attitudes.

Those who hold that the Bible is true are in effect distancing them-

---

5. Stephen T. Davis, *The Debate About the Bible: Inerrancy Versus Infallibility* (Philadelphia: Westminster Press, 1977).

selves from all such views as the preceding: they approach the Bible with a hermeneutic of trust. Anselm said: "I am sure that, if I say anything which plainly opposes the Holy Scriptures, it is false; and if I am aware of it, I will no longer hold it."[6] Such believers take Scripture to be the source of religious truth above all other sources, the norm or guide to religious truth above all other norms or guides. The idea is that all sources of religious truth are subordinate to Scripture and are to be tested by Scripture. Scripture has the last word or final say: whatever Scripture says (when it is correctly interpreted), goes. I take it that this is what the Westminster Divines were affirming when they wrote: "The Supreme Judge, by whom all controversies of religion are to be determined, and all decrees of councils, opinions of ancient writers, doctrines of men, and private spirits, are to be examined, and in whose sentence we are to rest, can be no other but the Holy Spirit speaking to us in the Scriptures."[7]

The opinion that the Bible is true depends on a certain view of its character, so to speak. It is not just that we take it to be Scripture — although we do (as if we could also take *Thus Spoke Zarathustra* or *The History of the Synoptic Tradition* to be Scripture if we wanted to). It depends on the view that the Bible is a special book, a book unlike all other books, a book in which, in some strong sense, God speaks to us. Those who hold that the Bible is true can never regard it as merely or simply a human product such as *The Iliad* or *Phaedo* or the works of Nietzsche or the works of Bultmann. They hold it to be the Word of God. God does not speak to us in the words of *The Iliad* or *Phaedo* or *Thus Spoke Zarathustra* or *The History of the Synoptic Tradition*, despite their status as cultural or academic classics. Or at least their words do not speak to us in anything like the same way.

---

6. Anselm, *St Anselm: Collected Writings* (La Salle, IL: Open Court, 1962), p. 220 (*Cur Deus Homo*, I, xviii).

7. *The Westminster Confession*, I, 10. See Part I, *The Constitution of the Presbyterian Church (USA)* (New York: Office of the General Assembly, 1983), 6.010.

V

In this connection, it will be helpful to refer to the writings of two of my fellow philosophers who write about the status of the Bible. Explaining what troubles me about their arguments — especially what they say about the various discrepancies and difficulties in the Bible — will help me develop my own view.

The first is Nicholas Wolterstorff's excellent and ground-breaking book *Divine Discourse.*[8] I fully accept and presuppose much of his argument; the item I will mention is the only major point where I demur. Wolterstorff wants to argue that the Bible constitutes, or can constitute, divinely appropriated human discourse (or that it can be rational to hold that it does). That is, God can be taken as speaking in the Bible. Wolterstorff notes that there are discrepancies between different narrative accounts of the same events in the Bible. But since God cannot speak falsehoods, how can this be?[9]

One of Wolterstorff's strategies for dealing with this problem amounts to a suggestion that the Gospels can be seen as analogous in genre and intent to Simon Schama's book *Dead Certainties.*[10] Ostensibly a book of history — it is about the controversial death of British General James Wolfe in the Battle of the Plains of Abraham near Quebec in 1759 — it is actually a work of what might be called imaginative history. Schama offers several quite different and even mutually inconsistent perspectives on this event, some from wholly invented characters writing wholly imaginary accounts; but they are all plausible given one way or another of looking at the actual historical evidence. Schama also makes invented — but again (according to him) plausible — claims about the inner thoughts and feelings of Wolfe at various points. Wolterstorff sees Schama as asserting not actuality but *plausibility:* he is saying that things might well have actually gone this way in 1759. Schama never suggests anything contrary to the

---

8. Nicholas Wolterstorff, *Divine Discourse: Philosophical Reflections on the Claim that God Speaks* (Cambridge: Cambridge University Press, 1995).

9. Wolterstorff, pp. 252-60.

10. (New York: Knopf, 1991).

available historical evidence, but he goes far beyond it at points. He is offering something like artistic portraits of Wolfe.

Wolterstorff wants to suggest that the Gospels are something like this: they are portraits of Jesus. In places they suggest not what certainly happened but what may well have happened. The evangelists agree on "the identity and significance of Jesus," and yet they disagree, for example, on whether the cleansing of the temple took place early or late in his ministry. In places the evangelists were claiming to report what actually happened; but in other places they were only claiming "illuminating plausibility" for their accounts. This viewpoint, Wolterstorff suggests, explains why the early church, aware as it was of the discrepancies, was so little troubled by them.

If I have caught Wolterstorff's meaning and not misunderstood him, I cannot agree. I am also aware of, and to a certain extent troubled by, the discrepancies between various narrative accounts of the same events in the Gospels. But if the Gospels are to be seen as similar in genre and intent to the book *Dead Certainties,* then I think the Christian church faces an immense problem. Unlike Schama's book, almost nothing in the Gospels as individual texts makes us want to think of them in this way. (I say "almost nothing" because I agree with Wolterstorff, Eusebius, and Papias that Mark was not much concerned with issues of chronology.) Indeed, I think it is about as clear as anything can be that the evangelists believed — and wanted us to believe — that *this is how things actually happened.* That is, they all seem to be making factual assertions about what Jesus said and did and what happened to him.

I suspect that Wolterstorff feels moved to make his proposal because he is comparing the several Gospels and not looking at the individual Gospels or their pericopes. And, of course, there is nothing in the world wrong with doing that. But perhaps there are other and better responses to the discrepancies than this. One would be to deny that they are there, that is, to try to harmonize the discrepant accounts. In the case of many of the discrepancies, I believe this enterprise can succeed. Another response would be to deny that the discrepancies matter much, since none (or none of the discrepancies that cannot sensibly be harmonized) seems to affect any crucial area of Christian belief or practice. Another response would be to affirm inspiration, infallibility, and maybe even inerrancy — but to arrive at a way of understanding those notions that is not undermined by occasional discrepancies. Another response would be to claim that the discrepant accounts mean different things, which is what Philo did with discrepancies in the Hebrew Bible and what certain church fathers of the Alexandrian school did with discrepancies in the New Testament.

I said that adopting Wolterstorff's proposal would present the Christian church with a big problem. This is because his proposal would require a hermeneutic for distinguishing between those Gospel texts that are meant as actualities and those that are meant only as plausibilities. But surely the radical interpreters of Christianity — to whom I, for one, want to give little ground — will claim, for example, that the resurrection of Jesus from the dead was not meant to be an actuality. How will we refute such people? I suppose by showing them that the chapters at the end of the Gospels simply do not read that way: that is, the evangelists thought of themselves as reporting sober fact. But surely that is true of just about everything we find in the Gospels (again, with the possible exception of Mark's chronology, Luke's grouping together of episodes with similar themes, and so forth). I cannot see how the job can possibly be done.

Rather than offering a useful interpretive tool, Wolterstorff's distinction between those accounts that the Gospel writers intended as true and those that they intended only as plausible seems almost impossible to apply to individual texts. How will we be able to tell where a given text fits? Moreover, the distinction can easily play into the hands of those interpreters who deny the literal truth of points that I, at least, consider crucial (e.g., that Jesus really was raised from the dead).

VI

The second scholar whose views I want to explore briefly is Mark Wallace.[11] So far as I can tell, he and I are miles apart on several important philosophical issues. I am much more inclined to embrace realist notions

11. See Chapter 4 in this volume.

of truth than he is. And although I would never want to de-emphasize the interaction between the Bible and its reader, I see the act of interpretation primarily (not entirely) as the discovery of something that is there in the text rather than the creation of something new.

To put the point crudely, Wallace is concerned that there is both good content and bad content in the Bible. The good content is constituted, presumably, by the teachings and example of Jesus and the high ethical teachings found elsewhere. The bad content consists of passages that picture God as capricious, taunting, violent, malicious, malevolent, and vengeful, for example, the God of the stories of Job, the Passover, and Ananias and Sapphira. Wallace's sensitivity to this issue leads him to see "truth" in relation to the Bible as something that is made or created (by the Bible *and* its reader) rather than something that is found in the Bible.

As I understand Wallace's argument, biblical truth exists (presumably exists *for* someone — let's eschew originality and call her Jones) when four conditions are satisfied:

1. Jones reads biblical passage P;
2. In reading P, Jones is prompted by the Spirit to do action A;
3. Jones does action A; and
4. A is compassionate, benevolent, loving.

Now my central difficulty with Wallace's proposal is that, since what is defined is not a characteristic of the Bible but rather a result of an interaction between the Bible and a reader, it accordingly does little to preserve any sense of the Bible's uniqueness. Notice that almost any other piece of writing can be true in this sense — *The Republic* or *War and Peace* or *The Bhagavad-Gita*. Wallace's notion is insufficient to preserve what I think the Christian community wants to say about the Bible. His definition of biblical truth leads him to a larger, but closely related, notion of theological truth. In theology, he says, a belief is true "just insofar as it fosters a life of benevolent regard toward the 'other'." A theological judgment is true, he says, "whenever it enables compassionate engagement with the world in a manner that is enriching and transformative for self and other."

And here I only want to point out the real possibility that false theological statements (false in the sense of not corresponding to reality) might be true in Wallace's sense. Furthermore, two logically inconsistent theological statements might both be true in his sense. Indeed, it is entirely possible that some true (true in a realist sense) theological statements may be false in Wallace's sense because they never foster "a life of benevolent regard for the 'other'." Take an abstruse and long-forgotten statement from, say, eighteenth-century Reformed theological anthropology, for example, "Adam was the federal head of the human race." Assuming, as I do, that the statement is coherent, it follows that either it or its negation must be true in a realist sense. But it is quite possible that the true one — whichever it is — has never fostered any particular ethical attitude in anyone, and thus is false in Wallace's sense.

In short, even if we adopt Wallace's notion of truth and apply it to some biblical text, it is still an open question whether the claims made in that text (if any are made) are true in Aquinas's sense. In many cases, this is a question in which I for one will be deeply interested. For example, I genuinely want to know whether Jesus' claim "I and the Father are one" (John 10:30) is true in a realist sense, quite apart from whether the Spirit has ever used that text to induce anyone to act lovingly and nonviolently.

What are the other available options for someone who wants to claim that the Bible is true but is as aware of and sensitive to the troubling texts in the Bible as Wallace is? Actually, it seems that there are lots of possibilities. I have mentioned one already: (1) harmonization, where the effort would be to try to show that the character of God as apparently presented in the "bad content" texts is not really God's character; when properly understood, the bad content passages do not teach that God is violent or malevolent. Here are some others: (2) Two of my colleagues at Claremont College, John Roth and Frederick Sontag, simply grasp the nettle and embrace both the bad content and the good content: their view is that God is both evil and good — that is, God has a demonic side. (3) One might try to find a theological principle that allows one to subordinate the bad content to the good content, for example, some such notion as "the progress of revelation." The idea would be to argue that the bad content texts represent a lower or more primitive understanding of the character of God than the good content texts do; the good content texts accordingly are allowed to criticize and supersede the bad content texts. (4) One might engage in what might be called "theodicy": this view would argue that the bad content texts are not as bad as they look, that God was morally justified in killing Ananais and Sapphira, for example.

Most of us who are committed to some version of what Wallace calls "the infallibilist model" engage in arguments 1, 3, and 4 above. We try to find a hermeneutic that allows us to emphasize the good content over the bad content — which is, of course, exactly what Wallace does in his own way. And I see no reason for his worry that people who follow that path will fail to listen to the voices of suffering people or fail to allow them space to struggle with God or express their anger with God.

The central point is that not all texts of Scripture are of equal theological importance or relevance to various religious issues. I believe that virtually all Christians, even those who believe in biblical inerrancy, at least implicitly recognize this fact. If proper hermeneutical principles simply entailed lining up various biblical texts and treating them all equally, there would be no sense in talking about a unified theme or message in the Bible (as Wallace apparently wishes to do, given his notion of the "supreme Christological plot line" of the Bible). More ominously, if we were simply to line up texts and treat them equally, then the Bible could fairly be said to teach things such as the legitimacy of slavery, the subordination of women, or the need to sacrifice animals at the altar of the temple in Jerusalem. Christians have always sensed that certain texts take hermeneutical and theological priority over others.

It's clear that there are places in the Bible where the Christian community has found it difficult to hear God's voice. What is needed, in the light of the murkier nooks and crannies of the Bible (among which I would include the divine command to slaughter all the Canaanites [Deut. 2:31-35; 3:1-8; 7:2; Josh. 6:15-21; 8:25-26; 11:12], as well as Psalm 137), is what I will call theological exegesis. This is exegesis in the light of what the early Fathers called "the rule of faith," that is, the church's view of the overall message of the Bible. Any given text must be interpreted in the light of the Christian community's vision of the witness of the whole of Scripture. Of course, such a vision must always be viewed as fallible and amendable by future exegesis. Otherwise, the Spirit's freedom to speak to us in Scripture is curtailed. Nevertheless, that overall vision can be seen as a canon against which to test various interpretations of various texts.

We can see what this principle means concretely in the following three points: (1) the Old Testament is to be interpreted in terms of the New Testament; (2) obscure passages are to be interpreted in terms of clear passages; and (3) everything is to be interpreted Christologically. Many of the Psalms, the four Gospels, and certain of the Pauline Epistles (especially Romans and Galatians) are taken to be hermeneutically foundational.[12] Are they "more inspired" or "more truly God's word" or even "more true" than other texts? No. The claim is merely that they are more hermeneutically foundational to Christian belief and practice. Nor is this an attempt to find something helpful or authoritative in a book that one largely rejects. I disassociate myself entirely from any such view (nor do I accuse Wallace of holding it).

I take it that Wallace thinks that some such procedure is acceptable as long as we recognize that it is an act of interpretation rather than a discovery of the Bible's "original meaning." Certainly, discovering what one takes to be the rule of faith is an act of interpretation, one that in the early church involved strenuous effort, vigorous debate, and careful discernment. But I do not accept the idea that any proposal about the overall meaning of the Bible is simply a matter of our imposing a meaning on it. It is entirely possible that that meaning is really there.

My own Reformed theological tradition has always placed great emphasis on the sovereignty of God. One aspect of this sovereignty is that God makes choices throughout redemptive history that are free, even (so far as we can tell) arbitrary. God chooses Abel over Cain, Jacob over Esau, the children of Israel over the Moabites or the Philistines. And God is not required to account for those choices. My fear is that the parts of the Bible that are "true" in Wallace's sense reveal a God who is too tame, too much under our control, not sovereign, and not mysterious or "wholly other."

Moreover, the biblical concept of the wrath of God — an embarrassment to much of twentieth-century theology — is in my view an essential

12. Several of these points were suggested years ago by E. J. Carnell in his *The Case for Orthodox Theology* (Philadelphia: The Westminster Press, 1959), pp. 51-65.

part of the Bible's message. Indeed, I would go so far as to say that the wrath of God is *our only hope* as human beings. (The grace of God is also our only hope, but that's another story.) Once, when I was a child, the foreman of our family's ranch was showing me how to do something with a horse. He said, "There are lots of wrong ways — and one right way — to do this." I proceeded to do it in one of the wrong ways, and I paid for it with bruises, cuts, hurt pride, and some colorful language directed my way by the foreman. Similarly, there are lots of wrong ways and one right way to live a life, and if we live our lives in any of the wrong ways, we will have to pay for it. The wrath of God shows us clearly that it matters deeply how we live our lives. Late twentieth-century folk wisdom isn't true, for example, when it says that any way you choose to live your life is okay as long as you're sincere and try hard not to hurt anybody.

My conclusion, then, is that we need a stronger notion of biblical truth than Wallace provides. We need to know why anybody should read the Bible as opposed to any other book. One has the feeling that Wallace thinks the Bible is a worthwhile book to read because we can take good things from it, or (more fairly perhaps) because the Spirit can use it to make us act compassionately. But can't the Spirit use other books as well? Again, why the Bible?

In the end, I need to admit quite frankly that not all biblical problems can be solved. No matter what moves are made or arguments are presented, we will still be deeply troubled by some of them. In places, our belief that the Bible is true will amount to an act of trust. There are texts about which we will have to believe that they are true despite our inability to demonstrate that they're true or how they're true. We may just have to wait. And perhaps that is not an altogether bad thing. As it says in one of the most troubling books in the Bible, "It is good that one should wait quietly for the salvation of the Lord" (Lam. 3:26).

VII

Let me now return to my main argument. Discerning readers will have noticed that I have been saying two quite different things about the statement "the Bible is true." Let us summarize the trusting attitude toward the Bible that I have been discussing (submitting to it, considering it authoritative, holding it higher than all other sources or norms of religious truth, etc.) as "submitting." Now it is clear that I have been claiming both of the following: (1) when I say "the Bible is true," I mean "I submit to the Bible"; and (2) my belief that "the Bible is true" is caused by my belief that "the Bible is worthy of submission." There is no inconsistency here; indeed, I am saying both.

I have said little or nothing in this chapter about how one comes to know or believe that "the Bible is true." Some theologians have claimed that the Bible is "self-authenticating." This is not an expression that I would prefer to use, primarily because, following Calvin, I believe that some things do authenticate the words of Scripture. Calvin lists, as I would, the testimony of the church (which he mentions but de-emphasizes), the admirable properties of the Bible itself, and (far and away the most important) the inward testimony of the Holy Spirit.[13] I would define the inward testimony as that influence the Holy Spirit exerts on the minds of believers when they reach the certainty that God speaks to them in the Bible and that accordingly they must submit to it.

In closing, let me turn to an important point that I have not addressed thus far: the title of this chapter: "What Do We Mean When We Say, 'The Bible Is True'?" It is important to note that the question is in the first-person plural: "What do we mean?" I take the "we" in this question to range over the whole of the Christian community, past and present. That's why I want to emphasize a notion of the Bible's truth that honors what the Fathers called the "rule of faith," one that includes as many Christians as possible and as much of the past as possible. There are Christians, of course, with whom I cannot agree at various points, nor am I recommending slavish obedience to the Christian past. But as a Christian academic who has spent his entire full-time career at secular institutions of higher education, I find that this "we" has always been important and comforting. In the face of opposition or, more frequently, indifference from my colleagues, I frequently need to remind myself that my affirmation that the Bible is true is

---

13. See *The Institutes* (Philadelphia: The Westminster Press, 1960), I, vii, 4; III, ii, 34.

not an affirmation made by me alone. It is an affirmation made by the community of which I am part — the Christian community.

We human beings are verbivores: we live by the words that come from the mouth of the Lord. I have not committed myself to any particular theory of biblical inspiration in this chapter. However, I have affirmed that in the Bible we hear God speaking to us. When we hear God's voice, the proper response is submission, wonder, and praise. That God speaks to us in the Bible, and that we faithfully submit to those words, is what we mean when we say, "The Bible is true."

"I Am the Truth": An Understanding of Truth from Christology for Scripture

ALAN G. PADGETT

> Art . . . is the telling of truth, and is the only available method for the telling of certain truths.
>
> Iris Murdoch, The Black Prince

> The history of the nature of Western art corresponds to the change of the nature of truth.
>
> Martin Heidegger, "The Origin of the Work of Art"

We live in a world of many truths, which nevertheless hungers and thirsts for *the* truth beyond the shifting plain of human history. The postmodern and multicultural turn in contemporary culture has raised again, in a powerful way, the question of truth for any ethic or religion that claims to move beyond the particular. Truth is both abhorrent and attractive, despised and desired, condemned and lamented. What is truth? Who is it that does not ask Pilate's cynical question today, and in the same way seek to sit in judgment of Christ?

This chapter is about a confession, not a definition. What understanding of truth is adequate to the confession of the crucified Messiah as Lord and Savior — as *the* way, *the* truth, and *the* life? If only Christ could be tamed by our postmodern pluralism and capitalistic pragmatism, so that he could simply claim to be a way among other ways, a truth among other truths, then all would be well. But Christ will not be so tamed and caged. Jesus Christ is Lord of all, or else he is a fake. The teachings of Christ, and his willing self-sacrifice for the redemption of the human race (not to mention his victory over death itself), allow no compromise with religious pluralism. His own deeds and words will not allow another option, however much our "spiritual" age would like him to conform to its religious eclecticism. So I begin with a confession, with *the* Christian confession: the messiah Jesus is the truth and the way and the life. The crucified God is the resurrection and the life; there is no other who can truly save. In keeping with this confession, the church also looks to sacred Scripture as truth, and it finds Scripture to be true. In this chapter I will seek an understanding of truth that is adequate to this confession.

I do not seek a definition of truth, although I will mention some in passing. Rather, I want to stand under the truth and receive (understand) what light it brings. I do not seek to define, encompass, and regulate what truth is. Rather, I seek an understanding of truth that implies or suggests many working definitions, spread across many academic disciplines, in whatever art or science we find ourselves at work for the love of truth.[1] I am forced to use the word "understanding" because I think it may be less confusing than other words; but my use of it here is idiosyncratic. By an "understanding of truth" I mean something less than a theory of truth, less even than a definition of truth. In my work in epistemology I have come to the conclusion that the differing disciplines of academe serve different interests, arise out of different traditions of inquiry, and have different rationalities.[2] There are, however, commonalities across disciplines, and our common human reasoning does provide one area of commonality. There are analogies, parallels, and "family resemblances" among the rationalities

---

1. See Donald Davidson, "The Folly of Trying to Define Truth," *Journal of Philosophy* 93 (1996): 263-78. See also Bernard Williams, *Truth and Truthfulness: An Essay in Geneology* (Princeton: Princeton Univ. Press, 2002), ch. 4.

2. See the brief essay by J. R. Lucas, "True," *Philosophy* 44 (1969): 175-186. I discovered the essay by Lucas only after coming to similar conclusions myself; see A. G. Padgett, *Science and the Study of God* (Grand Rapids: Eerdmans, 2003).

of the special sciences. The workings of informal reasoning, for example, are similar but not identical in the various disciplines.[3] By an "understanding of truth," therefore, I intend this rather vague sense of truth across the disciplines. A more specific, definite, and clear definition of truth will need to be made within these differing (yet similar) traditions of rational inquiry. For this reason also, I do not seek a single and universal definition of truth.

The church needs to pay a little more attention to its own internal grammar and a bit less attention to logic, philosophy, and the sciences, in seeking to answer the question "what is truth?" This chapter is an exploration in internal and communal rationality, a quest for a Christian understanding of truth that may or may not work for others. I can only hope that such an understanding of truth might aid academics in other disciplines, especially those who are Christians, in seeking to understand what truth is in art, history, or biology. But such an effort in Christian scholarship is not my main focus here; rather, with many contemporary theologians, I seek to understand what truth means for theology (especially Christology) and the Christian theological interpretation of Scripture.

Christ the Truth: A Proposal

To begin with, I will simply propose that we understand truth as *the mediated disclosure of being* (or reality). Sometimes that truth will be mediated through everyday experience, or common sense, sometimes through the specifics of propositions. This concept of truth has its roots in Scripture and in Platonic philosophy. I find it in Augustine, Franz Brentano, and Martin Heidegger, all of whom were influenced by Christian and Greek thought.[4] The value of this proposed understanding of truth is its flexibil-

---

3. See the appendix on informal reasoning in Padgett, *Science and the Study of God.*

4. See Augustine, *On True Religion,* par. 36 (§66): truth is *quae ostendit id quod est* ("that which points to what is"), *De Vera Religione,* in *Opera, pars IV.1,* Corpus Christianorum: Series Latina, vol. 32 (Turnholti: Brepols, 1962), p. 230; trans. in *Augustine: Early Writings,* ed. J. H. S. Burleigh (Philadelphia: Westminster Press, 1953), p. 258. See also Franz Brentano, *The True and the Evident,* trans. R. M. Chisholm (London: Routledge, 1966); and Martin Heidegger, "On the Essence of Truth," in *Existence and Being,* trans. W. Brock (Chicago: Regnery, 1949).

ity. It allows us to find truth in art and poetry, in spiritual experience and religious worship, as well as in logic and science.

For me, the most important source for the understanding of truth as the mediated disclosure of being is the Gospel of John. Truth *(aletheia)* is a key term in the fourth Gospel, and here it is already linked for us to Jesus. This truth is not simply information but the reality of the presence of God. John the Baptist bears witness to the truth, but Jesus is the truth (John 5:33, 14:6). As Bultmann rightly remarked, "So truth is not the teaching about God transmitted by Jesus but is God's very reality revealing itself — occurring! — in Jesus."[5] Jesus is the truth because he is the Word made flesh: the reality of God's kingdom fully dwelling in a human life and body. Jesus is the revelation of God, the Word of God, mediated through human flesh and a genuine human life (death and resurrection). Jesus is the mediated (incarnate) disclosure or revelation of the being of God.

Here I fully agree with T. F. Torrance, who has argued for some decades for the importance of the *homoousian* of the Nicene Creed ("of one Being with the Father") as a key to the understanding of theological truth. In an important chapter on the nature of truth in his book *Theological Science*, Torrance rightly argues that we encounter in Jesus not the truth in ideas or words alone but the truth of God in the person of Christ.[6] I cannot agree with Torrance, however, in his Barthian Christocentrism (at least in this early text), which causes him to claim that all theological statements are true only insofar as they are rooted and grounded in Jesus Christ. While Christ is indeed the truth of God made human, and thus the fullest and greatest of all revelations and all divine truths, it does not follow from this that Christ has revealed all truth (even all theological truth) in his human existence.

We can affirm the position of Torrance and Barth, however, in a certain sense. As God the Son, the Word is indeed the *source* of all truth. This is because, as God, the Word is the creator of all being (along with the Fa-

---

5. R. Bultmann, *Theology of the New Testament*, 2 vols. (New York: Scribners, 1955), 2:19.

6. T. F. Torrance, *Theological Science* (Oxford: Oxford University Press, 1969), ch. 4; see the earlier work by Barth, *Dogmatics in Outline* (New York: Harper & Row, 1959), p. 26, where he makes the same point about Christ: "To know Him is to know all."

ther and the Spirit). God the Son, therefore, in the tri-unity of God, is also the source of all other things that are (all other beings). Thus we can say that the Triune God (including the Son) is in some degree the source of all truth, because God is the source of all being. However, the Triune God is not the only being who makes truth known, and so God is not the source of all mediated disclosures of being. Torrance, following Barth, is right in some sense: all statements are true only insofar as they participate in some way, however distant, in Jesus Christ. My concern is that this statement is so easily misunderstood to mean that all theology must come directly from Jesus — or perhaps from the Bible. All truth is God's truth, but truth does not come solely from the story of Jesus — the work of Christ — nor solely from Scripture. Theological truth can come to us in many ways and in various places when we have an expansive understanding of Jesus as the *logos* of God in human flesh.

So truth as the mediated disclosure of reality or being comes to us at various times and in many ways, including, for example, in poetry. Great poetry reveals much to us of the human condition, and thus it can indeed be a source of truth. To the extent that art reveals the truth, God is its ultimate source. Now certainly the life — including his ministry, death, and resurrection — of Jesus is the highest and best revelation of God. But while Jesus does reveal the heart of God and is of one being with the Father, Jesus is not the only truth. Rather, we should say that Jesus is the ultimate, final, and highest truth of God. This claim is compatible with the existence of other truths, known through other media.

I have proposed an understanding of truth, not a definition. Rather, I believe that explicit definitions of truth are best left to each academic discipline and tradition of inquiry. My hope is that the understanding of truth I propose will be broad and flexible enough to provide a kind of family resemblance for the slightly different explicit definitions of truth. Before turning to an understanding of truth for a theological interpretation of Scripture, I will give two examples — from poetry and analytic philosophy — of moving from understanding to definition.

True Words

Some theologians have been so enamored of the power and beauty of modern logic and analytic philosophy that they have sought to reduce all truth to true propositions. Torrance is correct in reacting strongly against this reductionism, for Christ is not a true proposition. As the quotations at the beginning of this chapter underscore, we need an expansive view of truth that includes art, religion, and ethics — as well as language. I intend those quotations to suggest a need for such a concept. Such creative arts as poetry or painting can and do convey truth, even though the truth conveyed in them is not often propositional truth.[7] For poetry and other arts to convey truth, that truth must be more than true statements. It is often suggested, for example, that great poetry gives us insight into the human condition. Thus we might say that great poetry, in some cases at least, provides us with truth about being human. This insight is mediated by artistic and symbolic expression rather than by means of propositions, and it delights us as much as it informs us. Enough has been said about how poetry conveys truth about being human to suggest that the understanding of truth we are developing here can fit the nature of truth in poetry. Poetry, then, can at times provide us with a mediated disclosure of being — that is to say, poetry can be true.

We must not, however, wholly ignore true statements. Both poetry and propositions can be true words. Furthermore, a careful definition of truth is essential to any fully developed epistemology; therefore, philosophers need a good definition of truth in statements or propositions. Among the various proposals in this domain, I have been particularly impressed by William P. Alston's work in his book *A Realist Conception of Truth*.[8] His critical review of various antirealist notions of truth, particularly those found in Putnam and Dummet, is exemplary. Alston is clear from the beginning about his concern for "the sense of 'true' in which it

---

7. While beauty does convey truth, beauty and truth cannot be simply identified. The common — but not universal or fully explicit — identification of truth and beauty mars an otherwise insightful volume by David B. Hart, *The Beauty of the Infinite: The Aesthetics of Christian Truth* (Grand Rapids: Eerdmans, 2003).

8. Alston, *A Realist Conception of Truth* (Ithaca, NY: Cornell University Press, 1996).

applies to beliefs, statements and propositions" (p. 1). He expounds and defends what he calls a "realist" conception of truth, of which the following is an initial version: "A statement is true if and only if what the statement says to be the case actually is the case" (p. 5). His terminology is to be preferred to the unfortunately named "correspondence" theory of truth of Bertrand Russell in 1912 — a metaphor that is most confusing.[9] In the last hundred years it has sent philosophers looking for something that might "correspond" to a statement, and that is not really the point.

If we accept Alston's minimalist-realist conception of truth — which is a version of the definition of truth found in Aristotle and Aquinas — what about the understanding of truth we have been working with so far? Here I can only hint at an argument that would take much more space to work out in detail. A true statement tells us what is the case. If we think of "what is the case" as "reality," then a true statement tells us something about reality. We could say that a true statement "discloses something about reality" to us. And a statement is always expressed in a language: a true statement is thus a linguistic mediation of being or reality. As in poetry, truth in propositional form is also a mediated (particular, historical, finite) disclosure of being. Of course, a statement is a particular kind of linguistic mediation, and truth for statements will deserve its own special analysis. But we can fit a realist conception of truth for statements into the larger understanding of truth that I am advocating in this chapter. That is the main point.

My discussion so far has been merely suggestive of the direction we might take in epistemology or aesthetics. I wish now to turn to the main issue, that is, truth in Scripture.

---

9. Bertrand Russell, *The Problems of Philosophy* (London: Oxford University Press, 1912). For a recent defense of the "correspondence theory" (and I accept the material substance of his arguments, if not the term itself), see Andrew Newman, *The Correspondence Theory of Truth* (Cambridge: Cambridge University Press, 2002).

Thy Word Is Truth

The Bible is the sacred Scripture of the Christian faith. It contains the holy writings of the Jewish people under the rubric of Hebrew Scripture, or the Old Testament; the witness of the apostles as the New Testament; and it materially contributes to the holy book of Islam, the Koran. Whatever the status of the Christian Bible in world religions, here we are approaching it as sacred Christian Scripture — thus as the book of Christ. This implies that the truth of Scripture is about our relationship with Christ, for a personal truth requires a personal relationship. In more traditional theological terms, the truth of Scripture is about salvation, understood as God's work in creation, community, and the Christian believer empowered by the Holy Spirit. Scripture is true when it mediates this relational, spiritual salvation-in-process.

The implication of this conception of the truth of Scripture (that it mediates Christ) is that the Bible becomes our guide to religious life simply because Jesus is our Savior and Lord. Hence I find myself very much in agreement with the chapters in this volume by Stephen Davis and David Bartlett, where I find corroboration of my suggestion concerning the truth of Scripture. Bartlett writes: "He [Jesus] is truth because he shows the Father. To know him as truth is to know that he is also the path that we are called to follow and the life to which that path leads. In other words, Jesus is the truth that reveals, the truth that leads, and the truth that redeems."[10] The Bible is likewise true when it mediates this personal truth to us. Davis declares in his chapter: "If we take the Bible to be true, we trust it to guide our lives. We allow our lives to be influenced by it. We intend to listen where it speaks. We consider it normative. We look to it for comfort, encouragement, challenge, warning, guidance, and instruction. In short, we submit to the Bible and place ourselves under its theological authority."[11] Once again, the understanding of the Bible as true because it mediates the living Word of God, Jesus Christ, makes sense of this claim.

10. David Bartlett, "Preaching the Truth," p. 116 of this book.
11. Stephen Davis, "What Do We Mean When We Say, 'The Bible is True'?," p. 90 above.

I need to say immediately that I am not suggesting that we find Christ in every verse of Scripture. Rather, I would argue that, when we read the whole of the Bible as canonical Scripture, Christ stands at the center of the canon of Old and New Testaments and thus at the center of our biblical theology. When we put together the whole teaching of Scripture, Christ provides us with a key to understanding God's Word, because he is the living *logos*. And in order for the church to gain a level of meaning in which it reads the whole Bible together — with Christ at the center — it will need to go beyond the original meaning of each text read in isolation. In an earlier essay I have argued that the church needs to reclaim for our time a fuller and more spiritual sense of the Bible.[12] Instead of the medieval four-fold sense of Scripture, I propose that we develop a three-layered approach to biblical interpretation, seeking the conventional (historical or plain) sense, the canonical sense (Christ-centered), and the contemporary (or applied) sense of the text. If the truth of the Bible rests on these holy texts mediating the reality of Christ to us today in the community of faith, then this same community will require a level of meaning that goes beyond the original intention of the authors. And by simply reading all these texts together, we do in fact go beyond such a conventional meaning — to a larger, canonical one.

If we thus accept the truth of Scripture as a Christian community, we will see the Bible as true — true because, as these texts are illumined by the Holy Spirit, God's Word still speaks to us today. But what about the question of historical reference? Can we be happy with merely a contemporary meaning that is divorced from history? The answer to this question, spoken to by theologians as diverse as Ernst Troeltsch and N. T. Wright, is that some "symbols" or theological truths disclosed in the text demand a real historical event behind them.[13] We must beware of treating

12. A. G. Padgett, "The Three-fold Sense of Scripture: An Evangelical Grammar for Theological Hermeneutics," in *Semper Reformandum: Studies in Honour of Clark H. Pinnock,* ed. S. E. Porter and A. R. Cross (Carlisle, UK: Paternoster, 2003), pp. 275-88.

13. See Ernst Troeltsch, "The Significance of the Historical Existence of Jesus for Faith" (1911), in *Ernst Troeltsch: Writings on Theology and Religion,* ed. R. Morgan and M. Pye (London: Duckworth, 1977); and N. T. Wright, *The Challenge of Jesus* (Downers Grove: InterVarsity, 1999).

the text in splendid isolation from history, for Christianity is a historical religion. At the same time, we should realize three relevant points: (1) not every narrative in the Bible was meant to be understood as factual history; (2) even when the genre of the text is history, we should not demand greater historical accuracy of these ancient texts than we would of other historical works of their time and culture; and (3) the truth we derive from a historical narrative in Scripture may not demand a historical reference. All of this is to say that, when we accept the truth of Scripture, we are not also accepting a narrow doctrine of inerrancy, which reduces truth to propositions. J. C. K. von Hofmann knew this already in 1860, in his lectures on biblical hermeneutics:

> The saving truth which Scripture proclaims authoritatively to the Church does not consist in a series of doctrinal propositions, but rather in the fact that Jesus has mediated a connection between God and mankind. In the assurance of this comprehensive truth the interpreter . . . starts his work with the expectation that everything in Scripture will be an aspect of this truth.[14]

A logical reductionist conception of inerrancy undermines the truth of Scripture. Still, the truth of some biblical teachings demands a reference beyond the narrative world of the text itself. Biblical truth in certain historical narratives depends on a historical reference.[15] The question of reference cannot be absorbed into the world of the text without losing the truth claims of the text itself. Of course, such texts do not have to meet modern standards of historical accuracy in order to convey the Word of God for us today. We can justly demand only that they make reasonable historical reference, given the standards of good history writing of their own time and culture. Yet the truth they convey in these cases needs to be rooted and grounded in reality, that is, in history. Examples of this would

14. J. C. K. von Hofmann, *Interpreting the Bible*, trans. C. Preus (Minneapolis: Augsburg, 1959), p. 76.

15. Patrick Keifert argues for this point, among others, with respect to the Gospel of Mark: "Meaning and Reference: The Interpretation of Verisimilitude in the Gospel according to Mark" (Ph.D. dissertation, University of Chicago, 1982), pp. 33-35, 291-95.

be God's liberation of Israel in the Exodus, the return of Israel from exile, and the crucifixion and resurrection of Jesus. If these events do not have some historical reality, then their truth is undermined. However, this is not true of the book of Jonah, for example, which was never meant to be a historical text. The truth of God found in Jonah does not demand that it describes a historical event: the truth in Jonah about human resistance and repentance and divine mercy is more like the truth found in the great artistic works of poetry and painting.

WE BEGAN with what looks like a simple question: what do we mean when we say that the Bible is true? In this chapter I have been arguing, not for a theory or definition of truth, but for a Christian understanding of truth that would be true to our confession of Jesus as the way, the truth, and the life. I have thus proposed that, first, we understand truth in a general way as the mediated disclosure of being (or reality). For theology, then, Christ is the truth because he is the incarnation (i.e., the infleshment) of God's very being: God the Son living a real human life. Second, the Bible is true because the Spirit uses the words of the human authors and editors to mediate the Word of God (God the Son) to us in and by means of these texts. The Bible is true because it reveals God and God's plan for the salvation of Israel, the church, the whole human race, and all creation. I believe that this is what we Christians mean when we say that the Bible is true.

Preaching the Truth

DAVID BARTLETT

In Frederick Buechner's early novel *The Final Beast,* the protagonist, a young minister named Roy Nicolet, makes a pastoral call on a new member of his church, Rooney Vail. Rooney explains her strategy for getting through the worship service. "She told Nicolet that she was no good at praying and the hymns were too high for her and she could never remember what his sermons were about. 'So I add up the hymn numbers. Somebody's got to do it. And if they come out even, that's good.'"

But then she confesses the deeper reason beyond her apparent distraction: "'There's just one reason, you know, why I come dragging in there every Sunday. I want to find out if the whole thing's true. Just *true*,' she said. 'That's all. Either it is, or it isn't, and that's the one question you avoid like death.'"[1]

Is the whole thing true? What is the "whole thing"? And how does the preacher own the claim, and make the claim, that the whole thing's true?

---

1. Buechner, *The Final Beast* (New York: Seabury, 1965, paperback 1967), p. 28. Karl Barth foresees Rooney's question in "The Need of Christian Preaching," *The Word of God and the Word of Man,* trans. Douglas Horton (New York: Harper Torchbook ed., 1957), p. 108.

I

If preaching is not only a matter of speaking the truth but also a matter of interpreting the Bible, then it is appropriate to begin with a key biblical text.[2] Pilate is puzzling about who Jesus is: "So you are a king?" Jesus answers him, "You say that I am a king." Then, I think, there needs to be a full stop in our reading of the text. It is not clear whether the next sentence explains what kind of king Jesus is or explains why "king" is the wrong category altogether.

Jesus says: "For this I was born, and for this I came into the world, to testify to the truth. Everyone who belongs to the truth hears my voice."

Then Pilate asks his famous question: "What is truth?" But the question doesn't show Pilate's touching inquisitiveness; it shows that he hasn't been listening. We are not surprised when he heads out the door before Jesus can say another word (John 18:37-38). What Pilate would have got if he had been listening is the claim that truth is what Jesus says, and that belonging to truth is belonging to Jesus. Truth is a person, and to know truth is to be committed to — to belong to — that person.

Jesus makes the claim even more explicit earlier in the same Gospel. This time it is Thomas who doesn't quite get it, so Jesus says to him: "I am the way, and the truth, and the life. No one comes to the Father except by me. If you know me, you will know my Father also. From now on you do know him and have seen him" (John 14:6-7).

To know truth is to know God (not to know about God); the way to know God is to know Jesus (not just to know about Jesus.) He is truth because he shows the Father. To know him as truth is to know that he is also the path that we are called to follow and the life to which that path leads. Put in other words, Jesus is the truth that reveals, the truth that leads, and the truth that redeems.

In the light of John's Gospel, the way to understand Rooney's puzzle about whether the "whole thing's true" is to understand it as a question about Jesus Christ, who in the context of John's Gospel is, almost pre-

---

2. On the matter of preaching as interpretation, see David L. Bartlett, *Between the Bible and the Church* (Nashville: Abingdon, 1999), pp. 11-17.

cisely, "the whole thing" about whom we preach. On other days and in other ways we may puzzle about whether the all-encompassing Christology of the fourth Gospel is the only light we can shine on the issue of truth from a biblical perspective. At the very least, let us grant that Christology provides the appropriate starting point for the preacher. When the preacher makes claims about what is true, she is first of all making a claim about who Jesus was, who he is, and what it means to claim that he both was and is.

Given that, we can sketch out some ways in which other "truths" may point the congregation toward that Truth.

II

However one wants to qualify, modify, or escape Karl Barth, I am not sure there is any escaping his claim that, if we are to point to Jesus Christ as the Truth, we are bound to puzzle about the truth of the biblical text. "[The Bible] is expectant of people who *in* its question will recognize their own question as well as God's answer — a final answer, which redeems, recreates, enlivens, and makes happy; an answer, which casts the light of eternity upon time and upon all things in time; an answer which generates hope and obedience."[3]

In the first volume of his *Church Dogmatics*, Barth claims that God's Word (we can also say God's truth) comes to us in three ways. Above all, God's Word is the Word incarnate in Jesus Christ. Second, the Word comes to us in the testimony of Holy Scripture: the validity of the Bible rests precisely and exclusively in the fact that Scripture points to the Incarnate Word. Third, the Word comes to us in the testimony of preaching. Preaching always points to Jesus, but it points to Jesus by interpreting Scripture. It is not the preacher's job to share his or her latest ecstatic experience or an important political and ethical insight gleaned from a thought-provoking journal article or a review of even the most life-changing movie or drama. It is the preacher's job to open scriptural

3. Barth, *Word of God and Word of Man*, p. 121.

truth, which (alone) can point us to the Truth become flesh in Jesus Christ.[4]

Barth does not reflect at any length on the interpretive strategies by which the preacher uses Scripture to point to Jesus. Drawing on Barth's practice, as well on his own careful reading of the history of biblical interpretation, Hans Frei has suggested that we read Scripture best as a history-like narrative. Rightly read, the narrative helps point us to Jesus.[5] Indeed, rightly read, the narrative indicates that Jesus *cannot* simply be the object of historical investigation, but as the hero of the story he is now alive and present to the reader.[6]

My own reading of Frei suggests that he takes it as a given that the Jesus about whom this story was told was a figure of history (indeed, I think that for Frei, with Paul, if Christ is not risen then our narratives are in vain and our faith is in vain); but other interpreters of Frei and of Scripture have wanted to hold that it's enough for the history-like narrative to have its own internal coherence and power without worrying at all about its extratextual referents. For them to preach the truth would be to preach a story that truly brought people to an existence that was rich and full, whether it was based on historically verifiable claims or not. (Put in Johannine terms, if the story of Jesus shows the way and enriches life, it *is* the truth, and there is nothing more that needs to be said.)[7]

---

4. See *Church Dogmatics*, Vol. I, Part 1, trans. G. A. Thomson (Edinburgh: T&T Clark, 1936), pp. 98-140. In his writing about preaching, though not in his preaching itself, Barth undervalues the way in which human experience, art, and even journal articles can provide a lens or a parable to illumine our reading of Scripture and therefore our preaching of Christ.

5. I take this to be the programmatic implication of *The Eclipse of Biblical Narrative: A Study in Eighteenth and Nineteenth Century Hermeneutics* (New Haven and London: Yale U. Press, 1974), which is itself primarily a history of interpretation, but whose hermeneutical suggestiveness is inescapable. On Barth and narrative, see also David Kelsey, *Proving Doctrine: The Uses of Scripture in Modern Theology* (Harrisburg, PA: Trinity Press International, 1999).

6. See *The Identity of Jesus Christ: The Hermeneutical Bases of Dogmatic Theology* (Philadelphia: Fortress Press, 1975). For our purposes, one can almost say that if you don't know that the story is true by the end, you haven't yet heard the story right.

7. Richard C. Prust, "The Truthfulness of Sacred Story," *Soundings* lxviii/4, pp. 479-92, comes close to this position, distinguishing his view from Julian Hartt's claim that sacred story still needs ontological (historical?) grounding.

Brian Moore has written a novel about a priest who believes that the story he preaches has a powerful capacity to improve the lives of the people who hear it. The trouble is that the priest no longer believes that the story is true, that is, that it has any grounding in history or ontology. As one who has preached for many years, often with careful attention to the narrative shape of Scripture and the possibility for narrative in the sermon, I confess to the suspicion that when people in the congregation drag themselves in every Sunday wanting "to know if it's true," they are wondering about something more than whether the story is helpful, though they do want that. When they hear Scripture, they attend to the text because they believe that it points to a God who is at work in the world and not only at work in the text.

All this is not to say that we devote the sermon primarily to questions about the historical Jesus or the historical Israel. On the whole, we tell the story. But we are honest about the historical questions the stories sometimes raise, because people want to know whether "the whole thing is true — just true." After all these years I still affirm the wisdom of what my teacher Nils Dahl wrote about the issue of historicity and Christian truth:

> That faith is *relatively* uninterested in the historical Jesus research does not mean that it is *absolutely* uninterested in it. To draw this conclusion would be a kerygmatic theological Docetism, or even a denial of faith in God as Creator, under whose worldly rule even the historian does his service as a scholar. The fact that Jesus can be made an object of historical critical research is given with the incarnation and cannot be denied by faith, if the latter is to remain true to itself.[8]

How do we then attend to the questions of historical truth (and historical-critical truth) when we are preaching the Truth incarnate in Jesus Christ?

My sense is that we neither ignore historical-critical issues nor harp on them. Preaching on miracle stories as good stories without noticing that they cause problems for thoughtful believers does not pay sufficient

---

8. N. A. Dahl, "The Problem of the Historical Jesus," in *The Crucified Messiah and Other Essays* (Minneapolis: Augsburg, 1974), p. 77.

attention to a problem that is genuinely pastoral as well as theological. When we puzzle about the role of women in the New Testament and in the church today, it is not only honest but helpful to make distinctions between the undisputed Pauline letters and the disputed ones.

In this apparently postmodern world, I detect among preachers and theologians an occasional note of nostalgia for the premodern world, one where the Enlightenment had not yet reared its ugly head. How fortunate were Augustine and Chrysostom simply to move to allegory without puzzling about historical-critical questions — and might we not do the same? My own sense is that we can learn from them but cannot imitate them. We don't get to decide on the *Geist* of our *Zeit*, and if the reign of the Enlightenment is in question, what I think is unquestioned is that we have to go on from the Enlightenment, not back before it. And our parishioners surely think there is a difference between fact and interpretation, no matter how often we remind them of the subjectivity of every account.

If we do not acknowledge the role of "myth" and "legend" in the shaping of sacred story, our truth is perhaps not sufficiently truthful. If we think the whole thing is a splendid myth or an edifying legend, without reflecting the real God at work through a real man in the real history of the real world, we should perhaps consider another line of work.

III

If Christ is the truth, then we bear witness to that not only by the way we talk about the text but by the way we tell the truth about contemporary life, contemporary lives. If Barth is the great reminder that we cannot get to Jesus apart from the text, Kierkegaard is the great reminder that we cannot get to Jesus unless we choose to get there. Christian truth involves the Christian. In one of his discourses, a kind of unpreached sermon, Kierkegaard is talking about the kind of truth sometimes represented by the Bible, here by a verse from Ecclesiastes:

> There is a truth whose greatness, whose sublimity, we are accustomed to extol by saying that it is an *objective* truth, that it is equally valid

whether anyone accepts it or not, indifferent to the special circumstances of the individual. . . .

There is another kind of truth, or if this is more unassuming, another kind of truths, which we might call the *concerned* truths. Their life is not so exalted, perhaps because abashed, as it were, they are themselves conscious that they are not quite appropriate for all general occasions, but only specially for individual occasions. They are not indifferent to the particular condition of the individual. . . .

Such a truth is not indifferent as to how the individual accepts it, whether he appropriates it with his whole heart, or whether it merely becomes idle words for him, for this difference proves exactly whether he is jealous for himself. . . . Such a concerned truth is not indifferent as to who has proclaimed it; on the contrary he continues to be constantly present with it, in order that it may again concern itself about the individual.[9]

Steven Emmanuel sums up Kierkegaard's claim: "Briefly stated, he maintained that Christianity, as a human activity, involves more than merely believing certain propositions about matters of fact. The doctrines of Christianity take on a true religious significance only when they are given the power to transform the lives of those who accept them; only when they are given expression in the existence of the believer."[10]

This emphasis on the centrality of lived truth for Christian faith suggests three ways in which the preacher may make claims about the truth, claims that still point to Jesus as Truth incarnate. First, there is the appropriate place for the preacher to speak of the truth of his or her life. Buechner writes about his own practice as preacher and theologian: "What I started trying to do as a writer and as a preacher was more and more to draw on my own experience not just as a source of plot, character, illustration, but as a source of truth."[11] Certainly more than any well-

9. "Remember Now Thy Creator in the Days of Thy Youth," in Soren Kierkegaard, *Edifying Discourses, A Selection*, ed. Paul L. Holmer (London: Collins, 1974), pp. 95-96.

10. Steven M. Emmanuel, "Kierkegaard on Doctrine: A Post-Modern Interpretation," *Religious Studies* 25 (1989): 363.

11. Buechner, *Now and Then* (San Francisco: Harper & Row, 1983), p. 87; quoted in Marjo-

known preacher of our time, Buechner has used the stuff of his own life as the source for his homiletical and theological claims. He even revisits the same experience (notably his father's suicide) in different writings, making strikingly clear that the same experience is not precisely the same experience when it is remembered in the shifting contexts of the preacher's own life.

The biblical model for confessional preaching is St. Paul, who was not afraid to use the stuff of his own story as an exemplification of the gospel: weakness and grace in his own life re-embodied and refigured Cross and Resurrection. His story was not Jesus' story, but apart from Jesus' story his story would have been unthinkable. All of us grow weary of preachers who are at the center of every sermon, whether the story be one more travelogue through the Holy Land or a genuinely moving confession of terror and hope. But as one who more often hears sermons than preaches them, I can also testify that the preacher who distances himself from the claims he preaches about distances himself from the congregation he seeks to reach. The preacher's life is always a small embodiment of a great truth; but the great truth needs to be embodied in the preacher — sometimes explicitly.

More than that, the preacher helps the listeners look at their lives differently. Some of the best preaching tells a story that evokes recognition in the hearer: "So that is what repentance looks like. Not so different from what I long for in my life." "So that is the shape of grace!" On occasion I have even asked permission of a member of the congregation to tell a story she has shared with me. Events that provided a turning point for her often provided inspiration for others. Among contemporary homileticians, Christine Smith has been especially good at helping us think about the ways in which we weave the story of preacher, parishioner, and text together to convey the kind of truth that shifts lives — or turns them around.[12]

---

rie Casebier McCoy, *Frederick Buechner: Novelist and Theologian of the Lost and Found* (San Francisco: Harper & Row, 1988), p. 68.

12. *Weaving the Sermon: Preaching in a Feminist Perspective* (Louisville: Westminster John Knox Press, 1989).

And the congregation's life can also be named truly, both in its failures and in its possibilities. Again in his letters (and we can guess in his sermons) St. Paul is astonishingly willing to name names and to draw the implications of communal life. When is the Lord's Supper not really the supper of the Lord? What does the behavior of Euodia and Syntyche do to the common life of Christ's people? Why are the Corinthians themselves the only letter of recommendation Paul will ever need? What does it mean that the Galatians cry out "Abba" in their worship? Truth is not just proclaimed to congregations; truth happens among congregations, and truthful preaching is sometimes a great deal like truthful reporting — if the report is full of love and hope.

Here a word about the relationship between telling the gospel truth and telling the truth of the gospel may be in order. If the preacher reads the story of another preacher's visit to the beach with reluctant children, the preacher should not tell the story as if it happened to his family and him. If I gather from the Internet a pithy aphorism from G. K. Chesterton, I am welcome to present it, but not to present it as if I'd been poring through my *Collected Works* of Chesterton the night before. We do not need to footnote everything, but if my sermon title was one used by Edwina Hunter or John Claypool, I might at least begin by saying: "When another preacher used this title for a sermon, I liked it so much that I borrowed it for my own." There are all kinds of ways of signaling when we are borrowing without having to give the information more appropriate to a footnote than to a sermon. And there are ways of signaling when we are using our imagination and not our memories: "A certain man went down from Jerusalem to Jericho" is heard differently from "In 1987 my father was driving between Dayton and Cincinnati. . . ."

Here is an even trickier word. Sometimes it is not enough that an illustration be true unless it is also *truth-full*, not enough that it be factual unless it is also believable. Now this is tricky because many of the basic Christian stories may seem unbelievable to an age weaned from wonder. But I think we can steer clear of sentiment and bathos for the sake of believability. There is an awful illustration I have heard more than once about the train switchman whose little lad (always a "lad") was playing on the tracks just the other side of the railroad bridge. The father can either throw the switch and send the train and all that dwell therein into the briny deep or he can allow the train to forge ahead at the expense of his (undoubtedly) only begotten son. Even if this actually happened, it does not illumine the way real lives need to respond to the real God, and thus it is not gospel. It is *Guideposts* on a bad day.

IV

As we all learned in seminary, prophetic preaching is not really just preaching that makes people angry; it is preaching that is unafraid to name God in the world. One truth that preaching seeks to tell is the truth about human history. H. Richard Niebuhr has argued that to talk about God's revelation is not only to talk about God's word but also to talk about God's activity in history (Barth's insistence on the Word incarnate is not radically different from this). Faithful Christians do not necessarily see a different history from the history that others see, but we do read that history differently. Niebuhr makes the distinction between internal history and external history:

> In external history value means valency or strength. The objective historian must measure the importance of an event or factor by the effect it has on other events or factors in the series. . . . Not what is noblest in his sight but what is most effective needs to be treated most fully.
>
> In internal history, however, value means worth for selves; whatever cannot be so valued is unimportant and may be dropped from memory.
>
> As with value, so with time. In our internal history time has a different feel and quality from that of the external time with which we deal as exoteric historians. The latter time resembles that of physics. . . . In internal history, on the other hand, our time is our duration. What is past is not gone; it abides in us as our memory; what is future is not non-existent but present in us as our potentiality. . . .
>
> When the evangelists of the New Testament and their successors pointed to history as the starting point of their faith and of their under-

standing of the world it was internal history that they indicated. They did not speak of events, as impersonally apprehended, but rather of what had happened to them in their community. . . . They turned to a past which was not gone but which endured in them as their memory, making them what they were. So for the later church, history was always the story of "our fathers," of "our Lord," and of the actions of "our God."[13]

What is clear here and throughout much of Niebuhr's writing is the claim that the meaning of internal history is seen in large measure through the lens of what God has done in Jesus Christ.

True Christian preaching, therefore, is preaching that reads history in the light of the story of Christ, not to reinvent it but to re-view it as the scene of God's judgment and redemption. Even here, though, truthful preaching will require an honest description of the history we interpret. We will not reinvent history in the service of a homiletical point. A recent review of Stephen Ambrose's history of World War II suggests that Ambrose's patriotic vision has skewed his reading of the case.

Ambrose's view of World War II is similar to what Robert Penn Warren characterized as the self-righteous "psychological heritage" bequeathed to the North by the Civil War. Both engender what Warren called a "treasury of virtue" — a moral narcissism that can make us insufferable to other nations and can delude us into behaving like a crusader state. But the great problem with Ambrose's books — especially this one — is that they fail to treat history as tragic, ironic, paradoxical, and ambiguous. If readers are old enough to study an event that involved the deaths of more than 60 million people, they are old enough to learn that one studies history not to simplify issues but to illuminate their complexities.[14]

13. H. Richard Niebuhr, *The Meaning of Revelation* (New York: Macmillan, 1962), pp. 67-72.

14. Benjamin Schwartz, review of Ambrose's *The Good Fight*, in *The Atlantic Monthly* 287, no. 6 (June 2001): 103.

Of course we are not professional historians; of course professional historians will not all read the evidence or tell the story alike. But as truthtellers we are bound to tell the story as closely as we can.

One can see the dilemma even in Scripture. The books of Chronicles seem to rewrite the history of David and his offspring in a way that tempers the less-flattering portraits in the books of Samuel and the Kings. The book of Acts systematically — if not deliberately — plays down what the book of Galatians suggests were striking disputes between Paul and the church leaders in Jerusalem, including Peter and James, the brother of Jesus. Homiletically, one can see what is going on in both these cases: burnishing the throne in the one case; stressing the unity of the early church in the other. Honest preaching today needs to be honest about the God who works through history as it is, not as we wish it were.

In particular, truthful preaching will pay more attention to the understanding of history from the "underside." Reminders of Christian conquest too often understate the loss to the conquered. Suburban churches flourish while urban churches falter, and the rising and ebbing are not unrelated. This is a tough one to preach on pledge Sunday.

And we will not be naïve about the way material motives, especially economic motives, drive the world. The prophets (and Jesus) were unblinking in their ability to see that the lust for wealth was very near the heart of the human story. Christ became flesh in the midst of that material world. For example, why did the innkeeper squeeze in one more paying customer, and how much did he charge for the stable? How were the magi able to afford those gifts? Only a Gnostic God moves through an ether of pure ideas. The God of Israel and of Jesus Christ comes among the money-changers and the tax-collectors and the ivory palaces. Truthful preaching names that truth.

I confess to a dilemma here. For the most part, I have long maintained that the job of the preacher is to preach the text and not the (reconstructed) history behind the text. If Acts gives a one-sidedly optimistic picture of the growth of Christian unity, nonetheless it is Acts that we preach and not some scholarly reconstruction of the actual complicated history of first-century Christianity (where have all the Gnostics gone?). Nonetheless, one can also see how a reading of history that does not attend to the ambiguities behind the text can lead to a pious triumphalism. Most notably perhaps, the attempts of scholars such as E. P. Sanders to help us understand what first-century Judaism looked like to a first-century Jew have been helpful in getting us to recognize not only the understandable ways in which early Christian documents shape the story but the ways in which that shaping can lead to misunderstandings of contemporaneous Judaism — precisely because the story is more ambiguous than our preaching sometimes allows.

H. R. Niebuhr's "internal history" still demands reading the same evidence that the "external" historians read, and true preaching will sometimes take the time to look at Israel's history, the church's history, and our history with due attention to its complexity. Sometimes God is in the details, however much more fun it is to preach the broad generalizations.

V

I think truthful preaching needs to confront the established "truths" of the secular world as well. Perhaps it is because I have preached mostly in university settings that I have been painfully aware that questions of psychology and psychobiology, evolution and cosmology, do raise questions for our people, and preaching requires at least attending to those questions, even if we need to reframe them. Paul Tillich's attempt to let culture raise the questions and Christianity answer them was probably too neatly symmetrical for our time. But preaching that never attends to the intellectual world in which many of our people live runs the risk of quaintness and antiquarianism. Of course, our grandchildren will think that our attempts to be relevant are also quaint and antiquarian. St. Paul's borrowing from the Stoics and his arguments about angelic powers seem quaint to us, but they helped make his good news news to his contemporaries.[15]

15. For Tillich's description of his hermeneutical strategy, see *Biblical Religion and the Search for Ultimate Reality* (Chicago: The University of Chicago Press, 1955). For sermons illustrating that strategy, see Tillich, *The Shaking of the Foundations* (New York: Scribner's, 1948). In more recent years, David Tracy has examined the correlation between questions raised by

In particular, the issue of theodicy is raised in different ways within each generation, and appeals to the biblical world or the peculiar language of faith do not get us off the hook of saying something true when a child in the congregation dies, leaving her family bereft. We will want to say true things about God but also true things about the pain of the world and the hurts of our people — the truth that we are not built to last. The preacher who began the homily at the funeral of a young person by declaring, "What shall we say to this outrage?" not only got the congregation's attention; he was well on the way to speaking truth.

I am much impressed by arguments like those of my teacher and colleague George Lindbeck, arguments that suggest that the community of faith has its own language and its own rules for using that language.[16] But we are also, all of us, bilingual: we can speak Darwin and Freud and Peter Singer as well as St. Paul and St. Augustine. Truthful preaching requires the subtlety to speak both languages well, and to know where they can hold conversation with each other.

VI

Since I began with a brief discussion of one biblical understanding of truth, the one in the Gospel of John, I want to close by qualifying what I have said by calling attention to another text, from Ephesians: "We must no longer be children, tossed to and fro and blown about by every wind of doctrine, by people's trickery, by their craftiness in deceitful scheming. But speaking the truth in love, we must grow up in every way into him who is the head, into Christ" (Eph. 4:14-15).

This passage from Ephesians qualifies our attention to the truth of preaching in two ways. First it says what we have said from the start, that the shape of truth for the Christian preacher is defined above all by Jesus Christ. We test truth by what we know about him, and we speak truth so

---

the culture and the claims of Christian faith. See especially *The Analogical Imagination* (New York: Crossroad, 1981).

16. George Lindbeck, *The Nature of Doctrine* (Philadelphia: Westminster, 1984).

that our people may grow to be his people — his body in the strong image of Ephesians. The other truths that we declare serve what God has truly done in the man Jesus.

Second, Ephesians reminds us to speak the truth in love. This does not mean primarily that we trim the truth in order to be nice (though there is something to be said for kindness and courtesy in Christian discourse, even from the pulpit). It does mean that the reason we speak truth is a loving reason: the preacher preaches out of love for her people, and what she preaches is the love of God. There is no better way to love a congregation than to preach truth to them, and central to that truth is the love of God in Jesus Christ. It is not easy love or cheap love, but it is the love that shaped creation, fashioned the people Israel, was incarnate in the man Jesus, continues to sustain the church, and drives history toward its consummation. We speak the truth in love because we speak Jesus Christ — God's truth and God's love.

Biblical Truth and Theological Education: A Rhetorical Strategy

PATRICK R. KEIFERT

We have been asked to attend to two key questions about the role of the Bible in theological education:

> When we say that the Bible is true, what do we mean?
> What methods of interpretation appreciate the truthfulness of the Bible?

I propose to use a rhetorical strategy for attending to the question of truth and interpretive methods, one that, in a surprising way, confounds modern expectations about the speaker, the audience, and the ways in which the subject — namely, God and the Word of God through the norming norm of the Scripture — are to be present. These two questions drove the thinking of a course that Donald Juel and I taught at Luther Seminary for some fourteen years; and with these questions as referents, I have sought to address thoughtful Christian biblical scholars who want some starting points for helpful conversations about theories of truth and the teaching of the Bible in their classrooms.[1] This argument begins with the assump-

---

1. See the introduction to this volume; see further Juel and Keifert, "A Rhetorical Approach to Theological Education," in *To Teach, To Delight and To Move: Theological Education in a Post-Christian World*, ed. David S. Cunningham (Eugene, OR: Cascade, 2005), pp. 281-96; see

tion that the Bible is the Christian Bible, and, more importantly, that the Bible is Scripture. That is, as Scripture the Bible makes a claim about us and on us: our attention is not unidirectional, as if we alone are posing the question of the Bible's truth. Rather, we attend conversationally: God through the Bible also poses a question to us about the ultimate truth of our lives. To understand the Bible as Scripture, as rhetorical conversation, is not to deny that the Bible's truthfulness can be assessed in other ways — for example, for its accuracy as historical knowledge about ancient Near East cultures or as a source of anthropological data in these cultures. In theological education, however, the most life-giving questions we can ask are about the Bible as Scripture, that is, about what is being asked about the truth of our own lives.

Ethos and Speaker

Permit me to set the horizon within which I answer these questions as a way of getting at the identity of speaker in the study of the Bible as Scripture. As the setting for this conversation, I am imagining how I would begin a conversation with a classroom of theology students in a North American Christian denominational seminary.[2]

Theological education has its center in understanding God truly.[3] Yet,

---

also Keifert, "The Bible and Theological Education," in *The Ending of Mark and the Ends of God,* ed. Beverly R. Gaventa and Patrick Miller (Louisville, KY: Westminster/John Knox, 2005), pp. 165-82.

2. I currently teach classes that are largely secular in a private, church-related law school, as well as church-renewal training classes for lay Christians and others. In principle, there are significant similarities in the way I would confront the truthfulness of the Bible in a denominational seminary and in a secular private law school and in a church-related law school, even though my students' attention is not so directly focused on the question of the Bible as Scripture.

3. My debt to the work of David H. Kelsey, especially his *To Understand God Truly: What's Theological about a Theological School* (Louisville: Westminster/John Knox Press, 1992), is obvious. But unlike Kelsey's proposal, which is an extremely helpful space for a conversation about truth, this chapter reflects not a universal but a particular location for theological and confessional reflection on the question of biblical truth.

contrary to the expectations of some beginning seminarians who hope for some immediate and clear insight or transformative experience, to understand God truly we must often begin at most unlikely sources. Indeed, the looks on their faces when we make our first reading assignments tell us just how impossible it seems to them that they will begin to understand God truly in this classroom setting. But we must begin in unlikely places, for God is only known indirectly.[4] The simultaneously hidden and revealed nature of God[5] necessitates an indirect knowing, a learning that is accomplished through a set of practices.[6] These practices of knowing God largely grow, not within the self, for the self, and out of the self, according to the common wisdom; but they grow out of the congregation, that is, the face-to-face interaction of persons through the public practices of the Christian thing.[7]

Indeed, the congregation is the primal setting or location of all the practices that make possible the indirect knowing of God truly. Chief among the ways we practice the Christian thing is in worship, and for one important reason: at its center, worship as a practice reflects the Christian community's belief that the chief speaker in our conversation — the chief actor in our movement toward understanding — is not us but God. (Needless to say, Christians are also involved in practices of understanding God truly in other important locations. However, they do not function in the same primal way as the face-to-face gathering around word and sacra-

---

4. Kelsey, *Understand*, pp. 34ff.

5. Clearly, in this proposal I follow the Reformers, especially Luther and Calvin, on the hiddenness of God. I find B. A. Gerrish's analysis of Hiddenness I and II, especially in Luther, a most helpful framework for discussing the nature of this hiddenness. See B. A. Gerrish, "To the Unknown God: Luther and Calvin on the Hiddenness of God," in *The Old Protestantism and the New* (Chicago: University of Chicago Press, 1982), pp. 131–49. Luther's argument as pursued by Gerrish is in clear contrast to the various doctrines of God implied in indirect understanding found in other classic Christian figures.

6. Kelsey, in *Understand*, distinguishes four methods of Christian wisdom, or ways in the understanding of God: "contemplation, discursive reasoning, the affections, and the action that comprise a Christian's life." I develop these four ways, or methods, differently from Kelsey because of the particular piety out of which I teach Christian theology.

7. Following Kelsey, *Understand*, p. 32: "I will use the phrase 'nominalistically' simply as a place-holder for all communities of practice and belief who call themselves 'Christian.'"

ment does. These locations are indeed different in kind, for in word and sacrament God has specifically promised to be present as self-giving, self-sacrificing, liberating, justifying, and loving. God can, of course, be present to us in this distinct way in all times and in all places by the power of the Holy Spirit; however, the entire Christian thing is warranted by the *promise* of God's saving presence in the moment of word and sacrament.)

As the chief speaker, the chief actor, God promises to make God's self present as self-sacrificing, self-giving, liberating, justifying, and reconciling love.[8] God promises through word and sacrament to gather people and the entire creation into the triune life of God. In its broadest sense, worship is whatever one does when one is aware of the presence of the holy.[9] But for us as seminary teachers — and this is critical to our teaching of the practice of worship — Christian worship is whatever we Christians do out of the awareness that we are being called, gathered, and enlightened by the ongoing breaking-in of the promise of God's presence. We are thus the responsive audience in that rhetorical moment, not the One who speaks the truth. For Christians, consequently, while word and sacrament are central, worship cannot be contained in the formal liturgy of the people, in what we speak back in particular moments. Rather, worship continues as Christians encounter the word of God speaking to them in their everyday lives. This encounter, this listening, this worship is the Christians' *leiturgia* and *diaconia* — their reasonable service.

8. This list of metaphors for the presence of God is not exhaustive but it does include some of the central metaphors for the unique presence of God that warrants the Christian thing. Since the theory of truth out of which this proposal works especially reflects the metaphorical nature of the experience of truth, these metaphors are more than mere images of another thing, such as salvation — as if salvation is not just one more metaphor. Rather, these metaphors make present what they signify. As metaphors, they function as freeze-dried narratives or poems or prophetic utterances.

9. Here I borrow from a substantial philosophical discussion of worship, especially from the work of Ninian Smart, *The Concept of Worship* (London: Macmillan, 1972).

Pathos and Audience

Christian worship is always directed toward the world for the sake of the mission of God in the world. The practices that make up a true understanding of God, then, are practices that move us toward the world. So, for example, though meditation and contemplation of God are important Christian practices for knowing God truly, they do not lead Christians away from the world to some other place where God dwells, some other moment where one can be alone with God. Nor do other Christian practices, such as social action or critical reflection. All of these practices seek to de-center the self, to help the self recede so that we may understand God truly through the other. They are all practices that play on the biblical metaphor of hospitality to the stranger.[10] And they are all mediated through the written Word of God.[11]

The biblical metaphor of hospitality to the stranger suggests that, in understanding God indirectly, we experience three major de-centering moments, moments that again confound modern common sense about the "audience" for our understanding. In modern common sense, we who want to know or understand are the major actors, those who control the stage of knowledge or control the end of our rhetoric. Our conversation partners or the objects of our knowledge are, effectively, the audience for our understanding, the stage on which we move. When we are hospitable to the stranger, however, we are de-centered from our central role as rhetors, as actors by (1) the other, (2) the self, and (3) the Other.

The first moment of de-centering is perhaps the most obvious. When the self recedes in attending to the other — whether the other is Scripture, the Christian tradition, our own or others' cultures, the society around us,

10. My reference is to the many passages of Scripture wherein God is present through the stranger, the irreducibly other. For a more sustained discussion of this way of interpreting Scripture through its own metaphors, especially "hospitality to the stranger," see Keifert, *Welcoming the Stranger* (Philadelphia: Fortress, 1991). Of course, this formulation of the question of truth and Scripture is deeply indebted to the work of the Jewish philosopher Emmanuel Levinas, as my discussion in *Welcoming the Stranger* indicates.

11. This notice of the written Word of God leaves open the very important question of the relationship between the *viva Vox* and the written word.

the faces of the poor and the vulnerable, the call of the neighbor, the fellow creature, and so forth — the possibility of understanding God truly arises.

The second moment is less obvious, though equally clear if we think about it. When we are de-centered by these Christian practices, we also experience our own self as another.[12] The illusion that we are selves fully possessing ourselves, fully controlling who we are, evaporates. The common sense that life is a process in which we are finding or becoming or gathering together a single, unencumbered self proves a deadly chimera. The wisdom that the meaning of life is about "getting yourself together" for yourself proves foolish. The Christian practice of understanding God truly through the other gives us a new self, a self for the other, and a self as another. In my own Lutheran tradition, this is what we mean when we speak of Christian liberty.[13] If the moment of knowing God truly is the moment in which we experience the call of the other and of the self as other, then the nonsense that the Christian is the perfectly free lord of all and the perfectly dutiful slave of all begins to make sense.

The third moment of de-centering that takes place in the Christian practices of understanding God truly is the moment when we encounter God through the other. Within the Lutheran tradition this encounter is summarized in two ways: in any encounter with a fellow creature, we come before an irreducible other that gives evidence of traces of the Other who obliges us to be of service to that other human. In the encounter with the other in the shadow of the cross, we also encounter the mystery of the One who promises life in the midst of death, victory in the midst of defeat, and participation within the very life of God hidden in the everyday practices of the Christian's life.

12. Paul Ricoeur, *Oneself as Another* (Chicago: University of Chicago Press, 1992).

13. Martin Luther, *On Christian Liberty* (Minneapolis: Fortress, 2003). In this text Luther explores the metaphorical logic of the conjoined phrases "perfectly dutiful slave of all" and "perfectly free Lord of all," his way of understanding Christian freedom and faith. Note also the very helpful analysis that follows my line of argument in Eberhard Jüngel's commentary *Freedom of a Christian* (Minneapolis: Augsburg, 1988).

Practices

As the most obvious example, meditation and contemplation as ancient practices of understanding God are not an improvement on or substitute for the indirect knowledge of God. They do not do away with the necessity of engaging in other disciplines or practices of understanding God truly. They are simply among those practices. Contemplation and meditation are, to be sure, important practices because they bring together and overlap with the affection, passions, and primal *sensorium* of the human person.[14] In the tradition that I practice, singing a hymn until my self-consciousness recedes links the practices of contemplation and meditation to my primal senses. As I engage in a practice designed to help my self-consciousness recede, I meditate on the presence of God through the other and then contemplate God's presence in word and sacrament.[15] And if I choose a hymn from my Lutheran or another Christian heritage, hymn-singing also links my particular liturgical and theological tradition to older Christian practices of contemplation and meditation.

Social action on behalf of the poor and those most vulnerable is a similarly venerable and proven practice for understanding God truly. But social action dovetails with — even joins with — the ascetic practices of contemplation and meditation rather than competing with or excluding

14. Here my debt to Walter Ong's concept of the human *sensorium* is obvious. His concept also shapes the later discussion of ways in which the experience of the truth is shaped by the rhetorical events of Scripture in Christian practice.

15. The experience of the truth that is irreducibly that of identity in difference rather than identity in similarity is, then, irreducibly metaphorical in character. It is also the encounter of identity only through the irreducibly other. Here I follow both Paul Ricoeur, especially in *Oneself as Another*, and Emmanuel Levinas, *Totality and Infinity: An Essay on Exteriority* (Pittsburgh: Duquesne University Press, 1969), pp. 53ff., where he correctly, I believe, criticizes notions of truth based on individual autonomy that have dominated Western theories of truth. I also follow Robert Scharlemann's construal of the question of truth as "the experience of truth as a theological problem," in *The Being of God: Theology and the Experience of Truth* (New York: Seabury Press, 1981). While I recognize that these figures have significant differences on questions of the interpretation of the self and truth, the conversation they engender on understanding God and the questions of truth are for me the most fruitful for my overall proposal.

them. Perhaps the most profound lesson Mother Teresa left us is that so-cial action and ascetic practice are not different in kind or opposed to each other but of a piece — indivisible — in understanding God truly.

These practices or ways of understanding God are organically related to the practice of critical reflection, another way of knowing God truly. We moderns perhaps recognize critical reflection more readily as indirect, though the Christian tradition has not always isolated critical reflection as *the* indirect way of knowing God, as modern thought has taught us to do. But contrary to some claims about understanding God, Christians do not need to sacrifice intellect or discursive reasoning to understand God truly, nor to understand them as lesser ways of understanding. While the rea-soning intellect is only one of multiple intelligences that make up human understanding, those who would claim that it is somehow inferior or de-mand that it be excluded as a means of understanding God fall into a diffi-cult trap. They mistakenly assume that there is some method to construct boundaries between modes of human understanding without using hu-man understanding, which would seem impossible. Critical reflection is necessary to the exercise of all of the multiple intelligences that are God's gift to us for understanding God truly.

Within this horizon, Christian theological education both presumes and teaches these Christian practices that are the Christian thing. Chris-tian theologians invite critical reflection on and under these presumed and taught Christian practices. In my setting in a denominational semi-nary, and even more clearly when I teach in a secular setting, I cannot pre-tend that, when I am teaching about these practices while not actually practicing them, I am practicing the core of the Christian thing. For in my tradition that core is the movement of God toward the world in word and sacrament. I can, however, teach those practices and invite public discur-sive reasoning about which practices seem true to this understanding of God, and about how they can be adapted and instantiated to be true to that understanding. In short, a school of theology in my tradition cannot and should not simply presume, but should also teach, these varied prac-tices for understanding God truly.

Since the movement of God toward the world as self-giving, self-sacrificing, liberating, and reconciling love drives all my action in the world, it must drive my action in the classroom and my seeking for truth. And since the chief norming norm for all indirect evidence of God's movement toward the world through word and sacrament is the Bible, all my work in a school of theology must involve these practices related to the Bible. Notice, I have not said that the Bible is the object of my faith or its foundation. It is the norming norm of my indirect understanding of God truly. The question of biblical truthfulness, then, is not a separate question but a subset of the question of understanding God truly. I do not imagine that the Bible has some foundational status, not for persons of faith, much less for those who do not have faith in "the God who raised Israel's Jesus from the dead."[16] I do not seek to demonstrate its truthfulness aside from its place within my search — with others — to understand God truly.

My initial answer to the question "When we say that the Bible is true, what do we mean?" is quite simply this: the Bible is true insofar as it makes possible the understanding of God truly. In addition, in my own heritage this can be focused further by saying: "What makes Christ present" within our practice of the Christian thing?[17] Furthermore, those methods that appreciate its truthfulness are many. They include ascetic practices such as meditation and contemplation, singing, dancing, practices of social action on behalf of the vulnerable and poor, and the playful interaction of critical human understanding with text and tradition.[18]

16. Robert Jenson, *Christian Dogmatics*, vol. 1 (Philadelphia: Fortress, 1984), p. 99: "The gospel identifies its God thus: God is the one who raised Israel's Jesus from the dead. The whole task of theology can be described as the unpacking of this sentence in various ways. One of those produces the church's trinitarian language and thought."

17. Martin Luther's "was Christum treibt" — what necessitates, drives us to, delivers Christ (from "Prefaces to the New Testament," *Luther's Works: American Edition*, ed. J. Pelikan et al., 55 vols. [Saint Louis: Concordia and Philadelphia: Fortress, 1955-1986], 35:396).

18. In these last few phrases, my proposal owes a profound debt to the work of Hans Georg Gadamer, especially in his concept of tradition as *Wirkungsgeschichte* (history-of-effects), truth-seeking as interpretative play, and *phronesis* (practical reasoning). I have extended the concept of *phronesis* in my development of Christian wisdom. However, one need not draw only on the continental tradition, as I have. The work of Stephen Toulmin, especially his discussion of human understanding and the history of Enlightenment thought, is congruent with this proposal; see his *Cosmopolis* (New York: Free Press, 1990) and *Human Understanding* (Princeton, NJ: Princeton University Press, 1972).

✳

Second, truth is irreducibly metaphorical. All truth — even the supposedly univocal truth claims — rely on indirect understanding through the other. Truth, even as correspondence — and a correspondence theory of truth can be reclaimed by way of a second naïveté — is identity in difference, not identity in sameness.[19] The truth claims that Scripture makes on us take very different rhetorical shapes and strategies. We must attend to these rhetorical strategies and shapes to determine the kind of truth claim that is being made. Following a semantic, pragmatic model of truth would require us to admit that assessing the truth of "2 + 2 = 4" is rather different from assessing the truth of "I promise to be faithful to you." The character of those rhetorical strategies must profoundly affect how we decide whether our processes of interpretation and assessment are appropriate to the public, communal character of our conversation.

For example, in assessing the truth of a promise, an act of commitment, of self-giving, I would probably not ask, "Is the promise true?" (as I might about the arithmetic equation), or "Did it really happen?" (as I might ask about a historical event). Rather, I would ask, "Was the promise fulfilled?" This is a more important question for the biblical scholar, because the inherent logic of promise, especially the eschatological promises, dominates much of Scripture. Without simply reducing Scripture to a set of narrative promises, it is still fair to say that an assessment of the Bible's truth claims must depend on its truth claims to us and on us — on a response to the Promiser, an assessment of the faithfulness of the Promiser in fulfilling promises.[20]

Still other passages of the Bible function more as personal stories, as acts of self-disclosure and self-communication. In looking at these passages, we might more appropriately ask whether the teller's story coheres with what we know in other ways about the teller and about the world.

19. Robert Scharlemann, *The Being of God*, pp. 153–83.

20. Here I largely agree with Ronald Thiemann in *Revelation and Theology: The Gospel as Narrated Promise* (Notre Dame, 1985), and yet I part company with the Yale School's practice of projecting the rhetorical category of narrative on all of Scripture. I agree with the friendly critique Mark Wallace makes (see Chapter 4 of this volume) of Lindbeck et al., using Ricoeur's analysis of the primal rhetorical strategies of the Bible.

When the teller and the self-discloser is God, assessing the truth of the story involves assessing the story of all history, of all creation.[21]

As we recognize that the question of truth returns to us as a question that envelops and encompasses our own present discourse, we realize that we are unable to find some external, objective location or stance from which we can base our assessments. In practical teaching terms, this means at the very least that we cannot simply attend to some abstract "theory" of the Bible's role in human experience. Rather, we must centrally attend to the lived practices that will dominate theology students' peculiar role within Christian communities. Because my students are to be leaders in Christian communities of mission, I need to use interpretive methodologies to encounter Scripture that will teach them the skills appropriate to this leadership role.

As I have suggested, in the classroom I teach the use of Scripture as a way of understanding God truly through various Christian practices, particularly the practices of leadership. The interpretation and practice of teaching Scripture needs to embody a similar schema of practices and action. In addition to the venerable premodern traditions, I also try to provide a framework for students to use methods of interpreting Scripture in the modern period. I display these methods along a continuum, from the transparency of the text to a world behind the text to a complete opacity of the text to any reference — in other words, the text as self-enclosed world. Modern methods, in distinction to premodern and postmodern methods, are arranged from those that assume a high level of correspondence between text and referent to those that assume little or no correspondence between text and referent. When I teach students these diverse

21. This argument follows the work of my colleague Mary Knutsen, "The Holocaust in Theology and Philosophy: The Question of Truth," in *Holocaust as Interruption*, ed. E. S. Fiorenza and D. Tracy (Edinburgh: T&T Clark, 1984), pp. 67-74. See also Donald Evans, *The Logic of Self-Involvement* (London: SCM, 1963), revising Ricoeur's proposal in "Toward a Hermeneutic of the Idea of Revelation," in *Essays on Biblical Interpretation*. ed. Lewis Mudge (Philadelphia: Fortress, 1980). Ricoeur does not fully develop a semantic theory of truth in his attention to biblical rhetorical strategies and the kinds of assessments that stories of self-disclosure involving God might entail. His work raises the thorny question of how one might possibly assess the truth claims of a universal story that includes and encompasses our lives as well, including the part of our lives that is now engaged in talking with others about how to assess this story.

methods for interpreting Scripture, I differentiate those that explore the reference between the text and things behind the text (historical paradigm) from those that refer to things in front of the text (linguistic paradigm). I further divide these paradigms: I divide the historical methods between those who believe the text refers to events behind the text in the world of the ancient text and those who believe that the text can only truthfully refer to the world of the author of the ancient text. I divide the linguistic paradigm between those who focus on the rhetorical strategy[22] of the text and those who hold that the text reflects deep structures of the culture of those who wrote them and similarly the deep structures of the readers who interpret them.

By this time, it is no surprise to the reader that I invite students into interpreting Scripture through an imaginative free play around the questions of a rhetorical strategy.[23] As I have noted above, one practice of particular interest is that of public leadership in the church. This involves a specific rhetorical strategy on the part of the leader (student). Robert Terry provides an excellent heuristic tool for analyzing the present state of a community with respect to any question facing students and their ability to act.[24] Since the prejudice of my understanding of the relationship between biblical truth and interpretation is through shared action, Terry's focus on action fits my pedagogical purposes well. He describes six kinds of topics regarding action: existence, resources, structure, power, mission, and meaning. Within a community stuck on one of these topics, Terry shows how forward movement is to make progress in conversation leading to concrete action.

22. By using "rhetorical strategy," I deliberately avoid the habit of many biblical scholars to reduce rhetorical analysis to a genre analysis, a taxonomy of the text. A rhetorical strategy takes into account the shaping of audience, the disclosure of speaker, and the peculiarity of the speech. Thus, while narrative is a prominent rhetorical strategy in Scripture, even in the Pauline Epistles (since Paul presumes a shared narrative for his argument), the rhetorical strategies of Scripture are many, and they cannot be subsumed into a narrative analysis.

23. See further Juel and Keifert, "A Rhetorical Approach to Theological Education," cited above (n. 1).

24. Robert Terry, *Authentic Leadership: Courage in Action* (San Francisco: Jossey-Bass Publishers, 1993).

Terry's work on leadership can be more than a tool for furthering shared action. It can also be a helpful heuristic through which we might imagine the metaphors for the experience of truth within which our students can encounter Scripture in ways critical to their ministry of leadership. According to Terry, one way to imagine useful metaphors for the experience of truth is to think of a continuum: on one end are those practices that exhibit a high level of sameness, continuity, consensus, and agreed-on tradition; on the other end are those practices that display a high level of difference, discontinuity, dissonance, experimentation, invention, and innovation. For heuristic purposes, I imagine these theories of truth — now metaphors embodied in practices and actions — with at least seven zones of practice and action, as Terry enumerates them.[25]

These tools are by no means the only tools for the teaching practices that I believe are faithful to the truthfulness of the Bible as the norming norm of our understanding God truly. Indeed, I use several others. My point in sharing these tools is to show how I teach students to use — and to evaluate their use of — Scripture in leadership practices that allow them to integrate the substantial critical theory they are usually taught in school with the critical practices for understanding God truly. It frees students to integrate a diversity of venerable practices into their lives as leaders of Christian communities, and it undercuts the tendency for them to presume that discursive reasoning is at best irrelevant to leadership and that modern practices of leadership do not embody certain notions of truthfulness and ways of understanding God. Even more importantly, it makes a theological critique of such practices of leadership far more likely. In short, one extremely important strategic value of this approach, for me, is how it obviates the theory-practice split.

One other strategic value is the integrating of public and private practices of understanding God truly. In the modern period, the divide between public and private became common sense. The supposedly public ways of understanding anything were associated with "critical reason," which presumed an unencumbered self capable of placing all reasonable

25. Robert W. Terry, *Seven Zones for Leadership: Acting Authentically in Stability and Chaos* (Palo Alto, CA: Davies-Black, 2001).

subjects within its domain. This strategy follows a recognition that such presumptions on a certain mode of understanding are unwarranted and, further, that a much more particular, specific, occasional, and rhetorical mode of understanding is warranted as reasonable and public.

I have been advancing a specific rhetorical argument in this chapter concerning the Bible and truth. The question of the truth of Scripture does not occur in splendid isolation from the practices of the church, which seek to understand God truly. Understanding Scripture as the norming norm of life and faith within real congregations helpfully embeds various theories of truth for the Bible within larger rhetorical strategies for congregational leadership. Such an approach to teaching and learning about the truth of the Bible reveals that modern practices of leadership in the church do indeed embody certain notions of truthfulness and ways of understanding God truly.

Walking in the Truth: On Knowing God

ELLEN T. CHARRY

The Changing Meaning of Knowing[1]

Christian theology began life in a time of epistemic security, when God was believed to be real and some knowledge of him and wisdom through him to be possible. Under these conditions, the goal of reflection on God and the things of God was to understand them for the sake of a *good* life as well as *eternal* life. Theology rapidly became a philosophical outlook that interpreted Scripture and philosophical-spiritual traditions in light of the events surrounding Jesus of Nazareth, including reports of his appearance after his death that were interpreted as signs that presaged escape for others from death and the corruption of the body (1 Cor. 15). The goal was both (1) eternal life (in some form or other), and (2) a way of life that contributed to a just and benevolent community within a larger, hostile culture. Epistemic security about God is the normal condition for Christian theology of this primary, sapiential kind, which asks who we should become and how we should live. This primary, sapiential theology rested on an epistemology that joined knowing God to living rightly.

In a Hellenistic environment, knowledge is true if it leads us into

---

1. I am indebted to Jaroslav Pelikan's *The Idea of the University*, which was in turn inspired by John Henry Newman's *The Idea of a University*, for inspiring this essay.

goodness, making us happy and good. The idea that knowing good things makes us good implies continuity between the knower and what she knows. It is not simply to be cognizant of the truth but to be assimilated into it. Truth makes us good and strong, able to live well and so to contribute to healthy societies. Rational people will crave it because it helps them. Socrates and Plato were all about wanting to know the things that shape the soul in salutary ways for the sake of a better society. The purpose of inviting Athenian youth to love and pursue wisdom was all directed toward these moral-psycho-social ends. Paul, Matthew, and the Fathers of the church shared these goals. Primary, sapiential theology, then, seeks the knowledge of God so that we come to dwell in the truth; for the truth will make us happy and good, and in that way, free.

Several epistemological crises undermined this vision of truth. The first epistemological crisis came with the West's recovery of Aristotle in the twelfth and thirteenth centuries. Theology was pressed in ever more theoretical and less practical directions. It became an academic discipline for the purpose of suppressing heresy and sustaining the unity of the Latin church. The academizing or disciplinizing of theology separated the knower from the known and paved the way for modernity: knowing the truth became a matter of obtaining technical skills in the method of disputation. This distancing made normal theology impossible. Gradually, knowing something to be true took on overtones of acknowledgment and assent to what one judges to be the case rather than being an investment in understanding for the sake of becoming happy, wise, and good.

With this crisis, theology shifted from being sapiential and written for spiritual seekers to being academic, comprehensive, and written by and for scholars. Knowledge of God became possible on purely intellectual grounds, regardless of the piety of the theologian. The rationalist notion of truth was to get the ideas precisely "right" in order to avoid (doctrinal) "error," that is, to support orthodox doctrine that was the truth authorized by the church. Theological truth became encapsulated in logically articulated doctrine instead of what we would call existential engagement with God. It became an acknowledgment of some formulation of ideas as correct, whereas previously it had meant understanding things such that they made humans better, truer approximations of what God intended them to be. Truth became less personal and turned toward the analysis of ideas.

In the second crisis, during the seventeenth century, experimental science and empiricism transformed truth again — and therewith theology. In order to maintain — or perhaps regain — intellectual credibility, theology adopted the modern positivist and rationalist understandings of knowledge. These understandings separated knowledge from goodness (and therefore wisdom), and sapience remained at bay. Kant's critical philosophy severely limited the hope of knowing God, and so speculative philosophy was also dislodged from its privileged seat. Schleiermacher refined the medieval definition of theology in the service of the church in terms of ecclesiastical governance in his *Brief Outline of the Study of Theology*, yet again precluding the care of souls as a theological task. The modern disciplines and their subspecialties expanded the parameters of theology in ways in which its sapiential purpose never showed its face.

Theology turned from an interest in the good life, and the wisdom that forms persons in it, toward a narrower positivist vision of truth as either correspondence to events and facts or the logic of ideas without remainder. In short, the practical, pastoral bent of classical (normal) theology was defeated by the need to refute the diversity of religious belief in the Middle Ages and later by the need to sustain Christianity in the face of secular sensibilities. These powerful forces effectively separated knowledge from the knower and knowledge from goodness. In the face of these forces, the sapiential knowledge of God perished.

Now we are in the throes of a third epistemological crisis. Modern critical philosophical understandings of truth, knowledge, and goodness are on the defensive and, following the historical pattern, we may expect theology to adapt again, as its foundation shifts. From the limited vantage point that we have at the beginning of "postmodernity," it appears that theology may go in any number of directions, since what is called postmodernity is not yet epistemically clear. The likelihood is that, to the extent that postmodernity rejects truth, knowledge, and goodness, we may expect some forms of theology to follow this seemingly nihilist direction.

However, the nihilist stream of postmodernism is not the only option. Modern epistemology is also under investigation from a postcritical perspective that is not nihilist; this perspective is reconnecting the knower with knowledge and truth with goodness, so that knowledge of God may again be epistemologically possible. The recognition that knowing is a shared moral activity that requires excellences of soul can lend itself to retrieving truth that moves toward goodness — not in a sentimental way but in a way that truly recognizes our modern experience. The purpose of this chapter, then, is to explore how, given the current epistemological opportunity, theology might reclaim trust in our ability to know God and thereby trust in its primary, sapiential calling. To this end, I will begin by distinguishing the characteristics of theology under classic epistemological conditions, illustrating these by comparing small sections of theological work by Origen of Alexandria and St. Thomas Aquinas.

One further note is in order before we get into the argument. I am framing the problem under examination epistemologically because knowing God became a pivotal concern with Hume and in the modern critical philosophy of Kant. As I have already noted, modern epistemology separated knowledge from goodness, which distorted theology by detheologizing and fragmenting it. Now postcritical epistemology, which recognizes the dimensions of goodness and the communality of knowledge and truth, may help repair these problems — or at least identify a direction for repairing them.

We are still, however, a long way from achieving this, for three reasons. First, the discontinuity between sapiential knowledge and rationalist and positivist notions of knowledge is so great and so clear that it is difficult to appreciate the sapiential understanding that holds goodness and wisdom together with knowledge and truth. It remains readily dismissible as alien to our worldview. We cannot go back. Yet something was lost with the passing of transcendence and goodness from knowledge, to which the ensuing preoccupation with establishing the conditions under which theological knowledge may be possible has failed to pay attention. The price we have paid for freedom from goodness is the loss of companionship in the universe. We are utterly alone, and that is taking a psychological and moral toll on us. Here I will pursue the possibility of epistemological companionship as a way back toward the place of wisdom in truth.

Second, even as we reclaim goodness and wisdom in truth, the success and benefits of modernity's distinctive vision of knowledge and truth are so great and so deep within us that, despite the fact that it is now heavily criticized, we cannot get outside it. To a great extent, the modern vision is who we are. Furthermore, there are aspects of modern epistemology that we abandon at our peril. Modern empiricism and rationalism meant to curb authoritarianism, magic, and superstition, and that is something we must not forget when we attempt to address their weaknesses. Disentangling the strengths from the weaknesses of modern philosophical assumptions about knowledge is a delicate and daunting task (Dupré).

Finally, because we imperil ourselves when we abandon modern epistemology cavalierly, the current proposal stands within a modestly post-Kantian, postcritical option. Postcriticalism does not abandon modernity's insistence on evidence for knowledge, but it does recognize wider parameters for it. To anticipate a bit, beyond the admission of the personal into knowledge is the admission of the communal, moral, and psychological dimensions of knowledge that critical philosophy did not value. Let us now begin the argument proper.

Epistemological Crises and the Transformations of Theology

Theologians themselves have not reflected much on theology's changing rationale and mission in order to take stock of what theology is doing and how successfully it is doing it. Theological studies do not have a strong history of self-criticism. To attempt that reflection here, I will risk a schematic periodization of major transformations of the Christian theological tradition, with some help from Yves Congar and G. R. Evans.[2]

---

2. It is striking that I have been able to find only two works that track the changes in theology's self-understanding historically. One is Yves Congar's A History of Theology (1st ed., Garden City, NY: Doubleday, 1968), which traces important transformations in theology — and Catholic theology since the Reformation. He is concerned that important biblical cate-

What theology is and how it works have changed over time, with major shifts coming in the high Middle Ages and modernity. While both those divides named are of decisive significance, however, the divide between premodern and modern thought is of immediate concern. Despite the major transformation of theology in the high Middle Ages, the premodern age is largely characterized by what we will call "primary theology," while modernity is largely characterized as "secondary theology," though this second designation is not hard and fast. Primary theology has two forms, which correspond roughly to the two periods mentioned. Primary, or sapiential, theology began in the late second century (our representative will be Origen of Alexandria) and ran all the way into the seventeenth century, with figures such as Francis de Sales and Blaise Pascal. Yet, beginning with the twelfth century, institutionalized and professional academic theology created a second form of primary theology, namely scholasticism, later to be called "dogmatics." It was sustained through the seventeenth century, with a hiatus during the early years of the Protestant Reformation in the sixteenth century, during which theology was in a revolutionary rather than an institutional mode.

Secondary theology (theological scholarship) arose at the peak of Protestant scholasticism. It was a completely new phenomenon that effec-

---

gories — he lists "agape, flesh, know, *hesed*, justice" (p. 12), for example — dropped out of scholastic theology in favor of "a one-sided approach to Revelation that has considered it to be a collection of statements of a philosophical type dealing with realities which almost entirely escape our experience — as though it were a collection of theorems whose demonstration the teacher simply would not give" (p. 13). Congar's concern is located in the momentum of Vatican Council II, in which Catholic theologians succeeded in opening the church to modern liturgical and biblical studies. Congar invites Catholic theology to Scripture for inspiration to overcome some of the stultifying effects of scholasticism.

The other work, G. R. Evans's *Old Arts and New Theology: The Beginnings of Theology as an Academic Discipline* (Oxford: Oxford University Press, Clarendon Press, 1993), maps the creation of theology as an academic discipline in the twelfth century. She sets this back a century from the more common view that it happened in the thirteenth century as theology moved out of the monastery and into the school. Her argument is that secular studies pressed theology to academize in order to remain respectable and that the new status for theology achieved thereby enabled theology to become a powerful tool for suppressing theological diversity.

tively de-theologized large segments of theological studies and fragmented them into subdisciplines and guilds that now have difficulty conversing with one another because they look to different fundamental principles. The question is whether, in a changing epistemological environment, theology will be willing to examine its commitment to modernism in order to seize the opportunity to reclaim its normal (sapiential) voice and re-theologize itself. Such an attempt should not be mistaken for a sentimental return to premodern epistemological assumptions and styles; we cannot. But it may be possible for theology to move out of its marginalized corner and reclaim its distinctive calling to incite persons to a good and happy life by knowing, loving, and enjoying God.

The Transformation of Primary Theology

Before the seventeenth century, Christian study and scholarship were directed toward the knowledge, love, and enjoyment of God — that is, they were *primary*. Primary theology is only possible when the knowledge of God is believed to be possible, as it was until the European Enlightenment. Since all truth is ultimately unified and all reality ultimately connected, in the classic Western view, even if we view truth's various facets through different presentations and subject matters, all study and learning properly lead to the one truth of God. This follows from the teachings on creation and divine governance of the world.

Sapiential Theology

The first millennium of Christian theology was *primary* in the sense noted above, and heavily sapiential: knowledge was directed toward the goodness and wisdom of God, and it was the truth. Ascertaining what is true was a moral exercise in becoming good — or at least better; so the desire for wisdom (philosophy) was an attempt at self-improvement and the improvement of society, as Socrates taught us. In this, theologians followed their Greek and Roman predecessors, all being engaged in seeking a good life characterized by truth and beauty.

Gradually, the medieval scholastics began to work differently. Following Aristotle's interest in natural science, they distinguished, categorized, and classified thought for the sake of tidiness of understanding, presentation, and logical treatment. Modern theologians (those coming after the Renaissance and Reformation) followed this path. Psychologists categorize personality types, mental disorders, and therapeutic strategies. Biologists classify life forms. Similarly, theologians distinguish and classify doctrines. The goal of clarity of understanding thus becomes dependent on a classification system: things that fall outside these bounds become deviant forms of knowledge, labeled as quackery, superstition, heresy, and so on. The separation of mysticism from theology in the twelfth century is one example.

Following the late medieval and early modern adaptation of Aristotle, Johannes Quasten, in his monumental *Patrology*,[3] classified the writings of the Fathers into textual criticism, exegetical works, apologetical works, dogmatic writings, practical writings, ascetic works, and so forth — following the modern scientific paradigm. But, as helpful as classification — and, in its turn, typology — is for the sake of discussion, it has the effect of narrowing the reader's expectations of what she will find there. As they teach medical students: "If you don't look for it, you won't find it." As types are separated from one another, we read the works so categorized primarily in terms of these categories, and we may overlook or dismiss other things going on in the text. Such modern categorization tends to make readers think in anachronisms; the writers being so categorized did not think or write using those categories. A side effect of categorizing a work as dogmatic, for example, is to mute the sapiential dimensions of the text until they become invisible: they no longer count as significant to the interpreter who assumes that his own categories serve the intent of the author. Modern categories may impose alien terms on earlier texts, at least in the case of doctrinal studies. To understand a text well, one must try not to make it anachronistic, for the terms on which it was written may be broader than the modern categories can accommodate, not the least of which is its sapiential dimension.

3. *Patrology* (with Angelo di Bernardino), 4 vols., Christian Classics (Westminster, MD: Newman Press, 1950, 1986).

An example is the word "doctrine" itself. *Doctrina* in Latin (like *dogma* in Greek) means "teaching and instruction" in a broad, general sense and is used as such in Scripture and by Augustine in his *De Doctrina Christiana*. Its English form, "doctrine," came to denote a belief, theoretical opinion, dogma, tenet, or system of tenets in the late seventeenth and early eighteenth centuries. The current theological use of the term "doctrine" to designate both individual tenets and systems of tenets is a modern turn (the German *Dogmatik* is also a modern usage). Thus, to apply modern categories to premodern texts, while tempting, is also misleading: they simply did not have these categories. To reclaim normal theology — that is, theology directed toward wisdom and goodness — we have to repeal modern categories and follow maps laid down by primary theologians themselves.

The loss of a sapiential sensibility not only deadens us to an important dimension of ancient texts; it also blunts our expectations for our own scholarly and theological work that now follows the modern categories and genres that Quasten, for example, was using. Thus the primary goal of theology, to incite persons to good and happy lives, drops from view. When this happens, we anachronistically academize the premoderns, who did not know of such a task for theology, and we eliminate their concerns for our own day.

In his great treatise on the doctrine of God, *De Trinitate*, St. Augustine of Hippo transformed the pedagogy of classical culture for a distinctly Christian, spiritual use. (The treatise is exegetical, psychological, moral, ascetic, and pastoral, though Quasten lists it as dogmatic, establishing it as such for recent scholarship; discussing its ascetic, moral, and pastoral purposes must now work uphill against Quasten's authority.) Augustine is clear in his work that Scripture *(scientia)* is for wisdom. He makes the distinction in the concluding segment of Book XII of *De Trinitate*, which introduces the next two books — on knowledge and wisdom respectively. While he does distinguish scriptural support for the Trinity from the spiritual power of that knowledge, Augustine's point is that the former is not an end in itself but is directed toward goodness and happiness in God. For him, then, what Protestants later named "dogmatics" is the ground for the moral psychology that he develops in the second half of the work. Augustine explains that the *knowledge* we gain from Scripture is the subject matter for the lower mental functions; *wisdom* involves the higher mental functions. Wisdom requires knowledge but is superior to it: knowledge is directed toward wisdom, not vice versa. Quasten's categorization of this work as dogmatic is thus both anachronistic ("dogmatic" is a seventeenth-century Protestant term) and misleading — because the term does not capture the purpose of Augustine's work.

Congar interprets Augustine's vision of theology, and the layout of *De Trinitate,* by means of the traditional scholastic distinction between faith and reason, calling on two phrases — *intellige ut credas* and *crede ut intelligas* (which Augustine uses only once each in two sermons [45-46]) — to link Augustine's vision of theology to Anselm's and beyond into scholasticism, and to argue that Augustine adumbrated or perhaps initiated the scholastic distinction between faith and reason. But Augustine, who is always careful to tell his reader what he is doing, never uses a phrase link like this in *De Trinitate,* nor does he explain that its two halves represent theology and philosophy, as it has often been read. Edmund Hill, perhaps the current leading interpreter of this work, objects to interpreting the work via the faith-reason dichotomy; rather, it should be interpreted as "two consecutive steps in the only valid field of intellectual activity there is, which is the quest for saving, divine truth." Having rebutted the position taken by Congar (though not by name), Hill goes on to discuss the development of the various sections of the work forming an arc that he diagrams (27). He sees Augustine's distinction between "the lower function of practical intelligence or action, and the higher function of contemplation" (26), which characterizes Books XII-XIV; but he does not see that structure as the plan of the whole.[4] My suggestion is that this schema presents itself as the best hermeneutical key for understanding the work as a whole, and indeed for Augustine's view of the task and strategy of theology more broadly.

While the first half of the work is exegetical and explains the Trinity in light of scriptural testimony and dogmatic exegesis, the second half is psychological and explains how we are related to God because we are created in the trinitarian image that Scripture sets forth. Internalizing the scriptural

---

4. Edmund Hill, "Introduction," in *The Trinity,* ed. Edmund Hill (New York: New City Press, 1991), pp. 18-59.

teaching enables the reader to grasp it psychologically in order to assimilate the wisdom of God into his or her soul. Scriptural exegesis is to help the seeker discover who she really is; it is necessary preparation for learning wisdom and self-understanding in God. Exegetical and psychological interpretations together guide people to God and a healthy and pious way of life for a good and happy life. This pattern normalized theology as scriptural and dogmatic exegesis for the sake of spiritual nurture. The modern theological curriculum puts doctrine in one department and psychology in another. We may never understand what Augustine is trying to tell us about God and ourselves as humans as long as we sustain this artificial division.

Beyond recognizing that knowledge is directed toward wisdom, many of the premodern writers also had a mystical bent. At this level, sapiential theology seeks to unite the knower with the known, because partaking of the known is the knower's path to a good and happy life. Yet the mystical cannot be separated from the pastoral or moral and psychological intentions of the text, for these are all one, on the epistemological assumption that knowing something — or perhaps we might say *understanding* something — is to partake of it or to participate in it. The knower cannot be separated from the known. Intimacy between the knower and her knowledge began to unravel with the collapse of the Augustinian synthesis that led to medieval scholasticism. And this brings us to a closer look at the first epistemological crisis that academized theology.

Scholastic Theology

Sapiential theology guided Western Christians for over a millennium. However, imperceptible shifts began to occur in Europe during the ninth century that would eventually lead to the separation of knowledge from knower, fact from value, and truth from goodness. Here I will identify developments that bore directly on university education, for that was at first synonymous with theological education.

Education was revived in the monasteries in the ninth century, and the Dark Ages began to recede. Civilization had to be reconstructed for the survival of church and society. An important educational innovation came from the emperor Louis the Pious (776-840), son of Charlemagne, with the removal of the education of secular clergy from monastic settings to cathedral schools that were established under the auspices of the local bishop. Thus there were two venues for theology: monasteries and professional schools. This proved to be a fateful move. Rabanus Maurus even wrote a treatise on theological education, entitled *De institutione clericorum*, based on Augustine's *De doctrina Christiana*, at that time.

The next 400 years are dotted with moments of theological creativity, as Western theology struggled to regain its footing. Hildegard of Bingen, Anselm of Canterbury, the Cistercians, and the Victorines all wrote from the perspective of their monastic commitment. During the twelfth century cathedral schools began developing into universities, where law and medicine were studied at the graduate level alongside theology, and the monastery schools faded in intellectual importance, as Aristotle was translated into Latin. Evans argues that, pushed by the growing authority of the liberal arts, the twelfth century felt an urgent need to organize and integrate knowledge into an orderly pattern, partly to keep theology intellectually current and to extend and deepen its scope, and partly to refute popular heresies, especially those of the Waldensians and Cathars. Thus began scholasticism, the desire to tidy up theological expression for the sake of better organization and clarity. Peter Abelard pointed out opposing positions among the Fathers in his *Sic et Non*. Peter Lombard organized the theology of the Fathers thematically, relying heavily on Augustine, and set the precedent for treating theology comprehensively.

Abelard and Bernard

Professional academic theology was invented at the universities, where synthesizing and coordinating the wealth of scriptural, theological, and philosophical material they possessed became the task of theology. It required taking a giant step back from the materials themselves to do this. Organizing the material came to overshadow studying and being instructed by the texts themselves. This was the core of Bernard's attack on Abelard.[5] Evans argues that Bernard, the consummate monastic, was of-

5. Evans, *Old Arts and New Theology*, pp. 79-90.

fended by Abelard, who represented "the men of the schools which seek to handle with crisp decisiveness matter in which Bernard perceived mysteries too profound to be susceptible of such treatment" (p. 82). Bernard felt that the theology student had to be steeped in Scripture and the commentaries of the Fathers and had to understand them patiently. But Abelard was a technician of the latest modern methods, whose razor-sharp knives could slice incisively to the heart of a theological matter.

Evans makes the point that, while it may appear that Abelard was simply more skilled in dialectics than was the monk Bernard, who was steeped in Scripture, on a deeper level Bernard held out for being formed by slow and steady immersion in the texts of the religious life, rather than sallying forth with a sophomoric attitude after quickly absorbing methodological technique (pp. 44-45). At issue here is the fundamental sapiential question. Is theology a technique for promoting orthodoxy against challenge, or is it the formation of the soul for the enjoyment of God? Bernard, of course, was not unsympathetic to suppressing heresy. He supported the crusade against the infidels and testified more than once against those who, he thought, had breached the canons of orthodoxy. Though he was also a politician, his commitments were to the orthodox faith centered in the slow and deep immersion in Scripture and monastic practice. Evans concludes: "Bernard wants to prevent those who hear Abelard teach being blinded by his verbal and conceptual dexterity to the truths of orthodox faith" (p. 88).

St. Thomas

St. Thomas integrated Scripture, Aristotle, and the Fathers he knew, clinching the new vision of theology as an academic discipline that had been slowly forming since Anselm. Augustine, as we saw, also used *scientia* in *De Trinitate* XII, but with a quite different meaning: historical knowledge and management of daily life. With Thomas, following Aristotle's usage, *scientia* came to refer to rational conclusions attained through dialectical method rather than biblical testimony or knowledge in an everyday sense. For Augustine, scriptural and dogmatic knowledge was but the first stage of theology, whose goal was the wisdom of God that constitutes the deepest enjoyment of the human soul. Congar recognizes the moral dimension of the theological task: "The vision at Ostia is its immortal example and the *De Trinitate* contains its systematic presentation. To climb up to God in the Augustinian sense of wisdom employing research, the soul first uses its corporal objects, then the treasures of its memory which are its intellectual acquisition; finally it finds God in itself. . . ."[6]

Scholasticism was utterly different. It used a question-and-answer method that assumed there was only one right answer. One result of seeking conclusive answers to theological questions via dialectics was to make theology into not only a professional but also a competitive undertaking. One achieves success in the endeavor by defeating one's opponents in public intellectual combat: only one opinion emerges triumphant from the contest. Knowledge turns from being helpful to being correct.

Thomas also teaches that theological judgment is acquired through the standard human acts of cognition and by study rather than by the outpouring of the Spirit, as is wisdom (*Summa Theologica*, Ia. QI, Art. 6 [25]). Although the theologian must be a wise person, wisdom is of two kinds, he says: there is wisdom that results from having a bent toward judgment, and there is the wisdom that judges because one is versed in the principles of the field, even if one does not himself possess the virtues or the bent toward it. Knowledge as an objective, rational — as opposed to a spiritual — activity gets its proverbial nose in the tent here. My argument will take issue with the modern consequence of this move precisely at this point: I will claim that cognition is insufficient and that a virtuous bent is necessary for good knowledge. To state this theologically: grace is needed for good knowledge.

Knowledge of God and the things of God as precise, with the goal of becoming unimprovable, played into the hands of the newly institutionalized Inquisition, formalized by Pope Gregory IX in 1233, whose goal was to root out heretics from Europe and impose right doctrine throughout the church. The Inquisition drew its personnel from the Dominicans (St. Thomas's eventual order, though he was only eight years old in 1233) and

6. Congar, *A History of Theology*, p. 47.

the Franciscans. Perhaps unwittingly, though his work itself was at first condemned, Thomas's method became the intellectual beachhead for purifying the church. Doctrinal error subjected the errant one to excommunication and condemnation, exile, house arrest, and even execution by burning. The notions of correctness and tidiness for the sake of orthodoxy, while they were begun for apologetical purposes with Anselm of Bec and Canterbury, became the fuel for ecclesiastical power.[7]

The political story, however, is secondary to our interests. Despite all the changes that it brought, scholastic theology was still primary in the sense that there was clear epistemic access to God through revelation. However, Thomas also introduced the idea that faith is thinking that assents to propositions put to it, and this enabled assent to be "the whole nature of the act of belief" (*ST* II, II, Q2, Art. 1 [214-15]). By identifying the whole nature of faith as intellectual assent without regard for love, Thomas made way for the idea that faith is an intellectual assent to a set of ideas or doctrines — as doctrine would come to signify in modernity.

Thus the function of the truth of God shifted from wisdom for a noble life to an assent to intellectual claims arrived at using methods prescribed by and approved by the church. Fact and value became disjoined, or at least the possibly of their being disjoined appeared. Assent to true doctrine became the pathway to heaven, and it was seen as essential to the strength and power of the church. It is interesting to note that, as a tributary to these shifts, Thomas, in his famous "five ways," used the idea of secondary causality: God was the ultimate, or original, cause of things, but not necessarily the immediate cause. Although all knowledge leads to God for Thomas, distinguishing formal from efficient cause made room for natural causation, which would provide the basis for natural science to go its own way in the eighteenth century — without recourse to theological knowledge. Thomas, of course, could not have foreseen this consequence.[8]

---

7. Evans makes the point that the primary targets of academic theology were common heretics who opposed clerical power and the institutional corruption of the church (p. 138). The church also began a mission to convert the Jews at this time. Muslims did not at that point pose a social or theological threat to the unity of Christendom and so were left alone (p. 140).

8. See Louis Dupré, *Passage to Modernity: An Essay in the Hermeneutics of Nature and Culture*

Augustine had also needed to reconcile Scripture with philosophy. But he and other Christian Platonists perceived deep convergences between the reigning intellectual framework, which was oriented toward the good life, and Christian Scripture and tradition, which often helped them understand Christian doctrines better. When it did not, they either reshaped it to Christian need or simply broke with classical culture.

It is perhaps prudent at this point to offer a word about the Platonism that informs Augustine's theology. Platonism is endlessly pilloried for being world-, life-, and body-denying, and Augustine is endlessly browbeaten for ushering it into the church. While Plato's texts have been and can be read that way, the other side of Christian Platonism is that it offered a very optimistic view of the relationship between God and humans. Following Augustine's view, we can know, love, and enjoy God and find happiness in this life and for eternity by drawing near to him and making our home in his beauty, righteousness, and wisdom. It is our continuity with God through the Triune image that supplies us the dignity and courage to become our most noble and true selves. Augustine does not counsel self-deprivation, bodily suffering, or sexual self-denial, but counsels that we live into the spiritual truth of who we are as those made in the divine image. He took this aspect of neo-Platonism to encourage us to look up to God and then into ourselves.[9]

Thomas, on the other hand, was far more sensitive to the differences that he perceived among Scripture, Aristotle, and the Fathers of whom he was aware. Perhaps by then ideas seemed more rigid, flat, or self-evident than they did to the Fathers, who felt freer to employ words in novel ways and interpret ideas afresh, and to move back and forth among texts than did Thomas, engaged as he was in securing theology as the queen of the academic disciplines. The Fathers were experienced Hellenistic philosophers and were sympathetic to many aspects of Hellenistic culture. An important difference between Augustine and St. Thomas was that Augustine

---

(New Haven: Yale University Press, 1993), for an excellent discussion of this development, pp. 29-41.

9. Philip Cary argues that Augustine invented individualism by seeing the direction of spiritual knowledge as "in" then "up." I think a case could be made that Augustine is equally pointing us to go "up" then "in" as is the case in the Trinity.

did not have an authority to contend with such as Thomas had in Augustine himself — as well as the theological tradition of several hundred years. The Fathers themselves did not stand in an authoritative theological tradition the way Thomas did, because they were creating it; nor did they have to justify themselves over against one another. That intramural activity came only in the Middle Ages, when scholars had Scripture, philosophy, and tradition to cope with all at once. The Fathers had far more intellectual and spiritual room in which to maneuver than any theologians after them ever would.

Furthermore, the church of which they were a part was in a very different mood. In Augustine's day, the church was flush with confidence, as Roman civilization gave way to Christendom. It was in a darker mood in Thomas's day, hunting enemies in the long climb out of the Dark Ages. The arts were already disciplines that were defined over against theology as it had been practiced by monks, and the challenge of integrating disparate bodies of knowledge was sharper. The scholastics felt the urge to create formal intellectual, as well as political, structures to address questions raised to orthodoxy about God and consequent theological matters.

In sum, beginning with Abelard, scholastic theology used the liberal arts to turn theology into an academic discipline. By the twelfth century "no topic of modern academic theology had been left unexplored by the dialecticians, as if its subject-matter properly fell within the scope of an academic discipline."[10] This inevitably restricted theological inquiry to technically trained scholars, until theology was at best indirectly a sapiential art for those who craved God; mostly it became a professional and ecclesiastical tool for use against heretics and in the service of the Christian mission to "unbelievers" — Jews and, to a lesser extent, Muslims.[11] In the process, we see the beginnings of the infrastructure on which modernity would separate fact from value; it would also insist on the separation of knowledge from wisdom and the knower from the known, until the way these so-called opposites could relate to each other in the context of a larger whole

10. Evans, p. 27.
11. Evans, p. 150.

would become a problem to be addressed in its own right. At this point, rationalistic theology not only has a life of its own but a calling of its own. From the perspective of sapiential theology, theology is in an abnormal state, having been given over to technicians intending to solve logical problems — the bugs or glitches in the system. What has been lost in the process is the view that the purpose of the enterprise is not to create a smooth-running system but to train the soul to know, love, and enjoy God.

In effect, theology divided into two branches: professional scholarship done in the schools and wisdom for life with God, which became the province of "mystics" and monastics, including many women who, since they were denied scholastic training for the most part, continued the sapiential tradition of theology on their own. It continued in monasteries, the Cistercians being an exemplary expression. Their theology turned on the question of love rather than knowledge. St. Bonaventure, a Franciscan, was one of the few who masterfully integrated both orientations.[12]

Despite these decisive differences, sapiential and scholastic theology shared the belief that God exists and that knowledge of God is possible. Yet scholastic theology became absorbed with tidiness of presentation and intellectual justification, which took so much attention that the pastoral task of helping readers use the bare doctrines in their lives fell by the wayside; assenting to ideas, a far easier task, came to suffice. Having traced the transformation of primary theology from sapience to science, I will now illustrate the shift by comparing the first book of Origen of Alexandria's *On First Principles* (OFP) with the first several questions of St. Thomas's *Summa Theologica* (ST).

Origen on the Doctrine of God

Origen of Alexandria wrote OFP in Alexandria between 220 and 230 CE. Quasten calls it "the first Christian system of theology and the first manual of dogma,"[13] and he perhaps bases his categorization of the work as

---

12. See especially his *Journey of the Soul into God.*
13. Quasten, 2:57.

dogmatic on a passage that comes at the end of the preface to the work, where Origen identifies himself as one who seeks "to form one body of doctrine discovered from Scripture or by following correct [philosophical or logical] method." Quasten's categorization, using words (such as "system" and "dogma") that come from much later periods of Christian thought, again tends to set the modern mind in a direction that sees the text through categories that took on meaning only much later. Indeed, in his brief description of the work, Quasten does not see the ascetic theme that sets the tone for and runs straight through OFP. He even apologizes to his reader that Origen's writing "lacks coordination," is "too lax for modern tastes," and is too dependent on Greek philosophy.[14] Perhaps this apology reflects Quasten's unease with the integrated vision of theology that so energizes Origen. The latter's "problem" is that he is not a modern, for in spite of the hope of a body of doctrine, his is not unified by modern categories. Despite this astute observation — and perhaps more tellingly, by using terminology that comes from a later period — Quasten gives the false impression that theology across the ages is of a piece, with systematizing and dogmatizing perhaps its most sublime and sophisticated art form. This tends to obscure the losses incurred by the radical transformations of theology that we are highlighting here.

As I have noted above, Friedrich Schleiermacher has been designated the father of modern theology partly because he systematized, or tidied up, an exhaustive treatment of Christian doctrines and wrapped them around a single doctrine. In OFP, Origen is exegeting the three articles of the Apostles' Creed; but, though Origen works in an orderly fashion following the Creed, this should not be confused with the modern meaning of "systematic" as Schleiermacher constructed it — where all doctrines are reduced to a single principle.

The first sentence of OFP nicely illustrates how misleading the modern categories are if we use them to read the task of the work through the final sentence of the prologue. In this opening sentence it is clear that Origen is not working with modern categories. He holds together both the grace of God with truth and knowledge, and knowledge and goodness

14. Quasten, 2:61.

together with a happy life: "All who believe and are assured that grace and truth were obtained through Jesus Christ, derive the knowledge which incites men to a good and happy life . . . from the very words and teaching of Christ" (239a). The theological task, then, is to derive the knowledge of God that makes for a good and happy life for others. The task may also be to arrive at a unified presentation of doctrine, but this is not for the sake of preserving orthodoxy from error for its own sake; rather, it is the means to this further end of goodness and happiness. This is primary, sapiential theology. Modern categories, funneled through medieval theological history, would render Origen's practical task inconsequential.

Book I of OFP is about God. The reason for the untidiness in Origen that Quasten finds objectionable is that Origen cannot talk about either the scriptural descriptors for God or the unity of the Triune persons without explaining the practical-spiritual-ethical implications of these for shaping those who accept them. The reason to get it right — and not wrong — is for the sake of the moral well-being of Christians, not for refuting heretics or "unbelievers," or "truth" for its own sake. While these ought to coincide — and do for many theologians — the pastoral goal may ring unpleasantly pragmatic to the modern ear, which is trained to want "the truth," now understood as factuality for its own sake. To the modern mind, truth is fact without regard for value; but this was not the case for Origen's readers, who could never have severed goodness from truth. For them, objectivity would be an odd notion of truth. They knew of no value-free truth. For them, value and goodness were the essence of truth.

One of the main interests of Origen's argument is to combat thinking of God as a material substance or body. Origen shared this concern with Augustine, understandably, since they, like their modern protégés, were combating materialism. The reason for aggressively asserting divine incorporeality is not to enable Christian theology to comport well with Greek philosophical norms (that is, for intellectual credibility) but to orient the Christian soul toward its proper spiritual goal. God is scripturally aligned with light and spirit, and Christ is designated the wisdom of God, to teach us, not only not to confuse God with a material substance, but "to have it understood that the mind bears a certain relationship to God, of whom the mind itself is an intellectual image and that by means of this it may come to some knowledge of the nature of divinity, especially if it be purified and separated from bodily matter" (245a).[15]

St. Thomas on the Doctrine of God

Let us now turn to Thomas Aquinas on theology and the doctrine of God, perhaps the most famous single section of his writing. While Origen begins by telling us that the truth of Christ is to incite men to a good and happy life, Thomas's preface points us in another direction, because he has a different audience (university students) and works in a different setting (Christendom that is protecting orthodoxy in the face of heresy). In a brief opening prologue to the whole work, Thomas tells us that the *Summa Theologica* is "to convey the things which belong to the Christian religion in a style serviceable for the training of beginners" (I:3). In his case, beginners would be master's level students who already had sophisticated training in the liberal arts.

The first question, containing ten articles, defines the nature and extent of sacred teaching. It tells us that we are in a different world from Origen's, for theology is already on the defensive and needing to academize in order to hold its own. In this case, the liberal arts have the intellectual upper hand, and theology must prove itself worthy — or rather, superior. Origen had no comparable challenge, though he also faced a formidable alternative source of truth in philosophy and a popular one in common paganism. Perhaps the difference is that Origen saw epistemic continuity between philosophy and theology, and his undertaking needed no apology, whereas by Thomas's day philosophy already had the epistemic upper hand, or at least so his students thought, coming as they did flush with sophisticated philosophical training.

Theology, Thomas argues, is needed because philosophy does not treat

---

15. Augustine's great work on the Trinity argues quite similarly. It could be that Rufinus's Latin translation of *On First Principles* was available to him, although I am not aware of any direct evidence to this effect.

of revelation, and instruction by the latter is needed for our welfare, that is, for our salvation (Ia: 1). Furthermore, theology is a discipline similar to mathematics, only its first principles are not discoverable by reason as in mathematics, but only through revelation (Ia:2). Furthermore, it is a unified body of knowledge. Although its goal is action, it is nevertheless "more speculative than practical" (Ia: 4). Here is a further point of contrast with Origen, who is clear that theology is for the sake of a good and happy life that includes but is not limited to action. While Thomas finds theology necessary for our salvation, he ushers in the notion that it is a theoretical or speculative science. This adumbrates the separation of theory from practice that has been a continually baneful one for theological schools. In any case, coupling theology as primarily theory with belief as assent to that theory intellectualizes belief into a conceptual activity. It quite effectively removes sapience — wisdom for a good and happy life — from view because it centers on assent to correct church teaching to the exclusion of ascent to God.

In article Ia: 6, where he is still defining sacred teaching, Thomas asks whether it is wisdom, following Augustine's precedent that knowledge of God is the wisdom of God. Thomas is unswerving that sacred teaching is wisdom unconditionally. At the same time, for Thomas, wisdom is the skill of making prudent judgments, for "a person who possesses the habit of a virtue rightly commits himself to what should be done in consonance with it, because he is already in sympathy with it" (Ia: 6). Thomas understands wisdom as the highest of the intellectual virtues. While he wants to follow Augustine's teaching that wisdom is a divine gift of illumination, he actually follows Aristotle's opening of the *Metaphysics*, which views wisdom as practical reason: prudence, the ability to make sound judgment in a particular area of expertise based on a well-honed skill through practice, separate from grace or illumination.[16] This actually corresponds, not to Augustine's understanding of wisdom, but to his broad understanding of knowledge (*De Trinitate* XII. 22. 334). For Augustine, the wisdom of God is "concerned with things that neither were nor will be but just are, and which, because of the eternity in which they are, are talked about as having been and being and going to be without any change of real tense" (*De*

---

16. The citation is pointed out in the notes to article 6 of the Blackfriars edition, p. 20.

Trinitate XII. 23. 335). Knowledge belongs to temporal things, wisdom to divine things, as Thomas notes; but Augustine means by that, as I have noted immediately above, things that just are and are atemporal, not the sagacity of everyday sound judgment.

When Knowledge Is toward Wisdom

We have seen that intimacy between the knower and the known — we may now finally say between God and the soul — and the participation of knower and known in each other is the blessing of being known, knowing, and learning. God is blessed by our knowing him; we are blessed by knowing him. Research and education are inevitably instruments of formation (*paideia* and *Bildung*), probably close to what the ancients and mystics called contemplation. It requires being with, staying with, examining, and attending to something so that it yields to us as much of itself as possible. When we are blessed with understanding something well, it becomes intimate enough with us so that aspects of it cling to us. Perhaps this is what John's Gospel (14:21-23; 15:5-11) means when it talks about love and abiding, when Jesus says, "Those who love me will be loved by my Father, and I will love them and reveal myself to them." Love is not simply an emotion but is the presence of the beloved in the lover. Love leaves the fragrance of itself in the soul, just as sitting beside a glowing fire leaves its aroma on one's clothes, or embracing someone wearing perfume leaves a trace on one's body.

Something like absorbing the aroma of God is what the tradition means by contemplating divine things. Contrasting it with action is quite impossible, for once grace turns our face toward something, extracting the goodness that we can from it takes hard work, including strenuous preparation. Perhaps the classic distinction between contemplation and action is no more than being taken from that careful attending to what we enjoy and value highly to tend to other aspects of life's business that we enjoy and value far less. For we are able to delve into few things deeply enough so that engaging them is truly pleasurable and satisfying; and when we do, we may resent interference — even by necessary and important things.

If knowing well, sometimes gently and sometimes harshly, (trans)forms us through — and even at times into — itself, it is indeed true that knowledge cannot be directed other than toward wisdom or toward folly. It is not simply Augustine's suggestion that we should think so just because he was interested in the wisdom of God and because he is a weighty father of the church. The knowledge of which we speak here is wisdom: it is what remains in the soul after observation is complete. It is what stays with us after the impression that the encounter with the text or the lesson leaves behind — sometimes consciously and sometimes not. These insights nourish and expand us for good or ill. Not merely self-conscious learning, but even information-gathering may have its way with us.

It is an inadequate argument that sets forth an understanding of knowledge as one in which either knowledge passes through the knower, leaving no trace, or that knowledge is "out there," merely revealed or disclosed or located by the knower. Rather, strong knowing is a dynamic and interactive process in which both the known and the knower are constantly shaping each other. Good knowledge is directed toward wisdom, and bad knowledge goes toward folly. Knowing is a spiritual craft or art by means of which the soul grows by God's grace.

I am suggesting here that good knowing is to be taught by what one seeks to know. This is a moral and communal art that requires well-developed instincts and tendencies. When done well, it shapes the soul for a wise, good, and productive life. Good knowing is sapiential; it is only possible by divine grace. Therefore, a fuller way of talking about knowing will be to speak of it so that the skills and strengths of the soul are recognized. Learning happens in the soul. Locating knowing in the soul enables us not only to reconnect the knower with the known but also to see the connection between truth and goodness. Knowledge here is not information that one either has or lacks but has better or worse access to, depending on divine grace empowered by one's training and setting. Knowledge is stronger and better — that is, truer — to the degree that one's soul, and that of others, is enhanced or damaged by it.

Knowing God

Having identified the sapiential dimension of the art of knowing in general, we may now at last turn to the question of whether we can know God. On the terms put forward here, knowing God is not unlike knowing other things. It is a pedagogical task that is to be undertaken because knowing God is not knowing about God but an aptitude or skill of the soul animated by the gift of the Holy Spirit, as Christians put it. The classical attempts to prove the existence of God assumed that knowing God is unlike knowing other things and had to be demonstrated so that persons would see faith in God as a rational choice. Belief is understood here as the result of a rational decision taken against stiff odds. The assumption seems to be that, because we cannot provide scientific evidence for it, knowing God is unlike knowing anything else. When truth as correct ideas becomes important, these become the keys to heaven. The tendency in this direction began with Thomas when he identified faith as "believing with assent." Salvation became a cognitive activity: assent to correct belief (e.g., God is merciful to me) as determined by those authorized to determine it.

The sapiential point is not that, though we cannot prove the existence of God rationally, his nonexistence cannot be proven either, and so it is not irrational to believe that he exists, which continues the argument in terms dating back to Anselm of Canterbury's *Proslogion*. The point is rather that rational arguments that are forwarded, criticized, amended, and represented cannot enable us to know God — or anything else for that matter — so that we become wiser, better, and happier as a result, unless divine grace precede. The classical arguments are all pleading for an ostensibly special case on the assumption that reason alone, without prevenient grace, can arrive at knowledge of an exceptionally resistant target: God.

The problem with this whole approach is that it does not recognize that knowing God is an art of the especially blessed soul. It has locked onto the idea that such knowledge is possible given adequate information, what today we call the right-brain functions: the relational, psychological, instinctual, and inferential dimensions of knowing through which grace works have been eliminated. Cognatizing faith may not teach us the art of knowing God by which the Spirit enables us to become better, wiser, and thereby happier. Classical arguments all strain toward information that is difficult to convey, but they do not rely on grace to instruct us on how to benefit from the act of knowing. They have reached psychological and spiritual dead ends, for the cognitive aspect of knowing takes on meaning and a life of its own, leaving the wholeness of the soul behind. They try to shortcut a process that is not simplifiable, because knowing God, like knowing how to make a medical diagnosis, requires not simply "having" information but being in a sufficiently fluent relationship with that information to be able to use it skillfully. The self matures in the process.

Even flawless proofs for the existence of God will not work for many, because even the best reasons given for the existence of God must be translated into conviction, and that is a psychological event. A violinist translates notes into music, a physician uses test results to guard and restore health, and a financial advisor reads financial reports and follows the market in order to secure a comfortable retirement for her clients. All these require long-studied skills, until we finally say that so-and-so is a violinist, a physician, or a financial advisor. These skills are a central part of their identities. It is similar when they define us as being knowers of God: the experience of knowing God makes us who we are. God may be unlike anything else that we will ever know, but knowing him is not unlike other things that we know. The quality of knowledge in both cases depends on the bent of the mind seeking the knowledge, and that is a gift. As it happens with human lovers, it happens between God and us. By staying together over a long period, attending to their lover's manners, needs, and gifts, and being vulnerable to the other's very presence, human lovers become one flesh. If God is the one in whom we live and move and have our being (Acts 17:28), he is the one par excellence in whom we are. Knowing, loving, and enjoying God is another of those means by which, as St. Catherine of Siena put it, "he makes of [a soul] another himself."[17]

---

17. Catherine of Siena, *The Dialogue* (New York: Paulist Press, 1980), p. 25.

Index of Names

Abelard, Peter, 155-56, 160
Adam, A. K. M., 13
Alston, William P., 87, 109-10
Alter, Robert, 48
Ambrose, Stephen, 125
Anselm of Canterbury, 30, 40-42, 93, 153, 155, 156, 158-68
Anthony of Egypt, 46
Aquinas, Thomas, 55-56, 87, 98, 110, 147, 156-61, 164-66, 168
Aristotle, 14, 64, 110, 145, 151, 155, 156, 159, 165
Augustine of Hippo, 45-46, 65, 71, 73-74, 77, 106, 120, 128, 152-56, 159-60, 163-67
Austin, J. L., 45, 70
Avram, Wesley, 13

Balentine, Samuel E., 25
Barth, Karl, 44, 72-73, 75-76, 107-8, 115, 117-18, 120, 125
Bartlett, David, 5, 12, 14, 15, 111
Barton, John, 23
Bernard of Clairvaux, 155-56
Bernstein, Richard, 11
Bonaventure, 161

Booth, Wayne C., 8-9
Boyce, James, 10, 13
Braaten, Carl E., 59
Brentano, Franz, 106
Brett, Mark, 47
Buechner, Frederick, 115, 121-22
Bultmann, Rudolf, 75, 93, 107
Burgess, John P., 63
Burrows, Mark S., 65
Buss, Martin, 7

Calvin, John, 72-73, 102, 132
Carlstadt, Andreas, 53
Carnell, E. J., 100
Cary, Philip, 159
Catherine of Siena, 169
Charlemagne, 154
Charry, Ellen, 5-6, 13, 14, 15
Chesterton, G. K., 123
Chrysostom, John, 120
Claypool, John, 123
Compiers, Donald, 13
Congar, Yves, 148-49, 153, 157
Craigo-Snell, Shannon, 61

Index of Scripture References